COURAGEOUS WOMEN
OF THE VIETNAM WAR

OTHER BOOKS IN THE
WOMEN OF ACTION SERIES

———

COURAGEOUS WOMEN
OF THE VIETNAM WAR

───────── ★ ─────────

Medics, Journalists, Survivors, and More

KATHRYN J. ATWOOD

CHICAGO
REVIEW
PRESS

Copyright © 2018 by Kathryn J. Atwood
Foreword copyright © 2018 by Diane Carlson Evans
All rights reserved
First edition
Published by Chicago Review Press Incorporated
814 North Franklin Street
Chicago, Illinois 60610
ISBN 978-1-61373-074-4

Library of Congress Cataloging-in-Publication Data
Names: Atwood, Kathryn J., author.
Title: Courageous women of the Vietnam War : medics, journalists, survivors,
    and more / Kathryn J. Atwood.
Description: First edition. | Chicago, Illinois : Chicago Review Press
    Incorporated, [2018] | Includes bibliographical references and index. |
    Audience: 12+.
Identifiers: LCCN 2017040059 (print) | LCCN 2017040968 (ebook) | ISBN
    9781613730751 (adobe pdf) | ISBN 9781613730775 (epub) | ISBN 9781613730768
    (kindle) | ISBN 9781613730744 | ISBN 9781613730744(cloth)
Subjects: LCSH: Vietnam War, 1961–1975—Participation, Female—Juvenile
    literature. | Vietnam War, 1961–1975—Women—Biography—Juvenile
    literature.
Classification: LCC DS559.8.W6 (ebook) | LCC DS559.8.W6 A89 2018 (print) |
    DDC 959.704/3082—dc23
LC record available at https://lccn.loc.gov/2017040059

Interior design: Sarah Olson
Map design: Chris Erichsen

Image of Iris Mary Roser on page 96 and image of An Trong orphans on page 104
from *Ba Rose* by Iris Mary Roser. Every effort has been made to contact the copyright holders. The editors would welcome information concerning any inadvertent
errors or omissions.

Printed in the United States of America
5 4 3 2 1

Are you so smart that you truly know who's to blame? If you ask the Viet Cong, they'll blame the Americans. If you ask the Americans, they'll blame the North. If you ask the North, they'll blame the South. If you ask the South, they'll blame the Viet Cong. If you ask the monks, they'll blame the Catholics, or tell you our ancestors did something terrible and so brought this endless suffering on our heads.

—*When Heaven and Earth Changed Places*

Vietnam is like a huge jigsaw puzzle where none of the pieces fit.

—*Ba Rose: My Years in Vietnam, 1968–1971*

CONTENTS

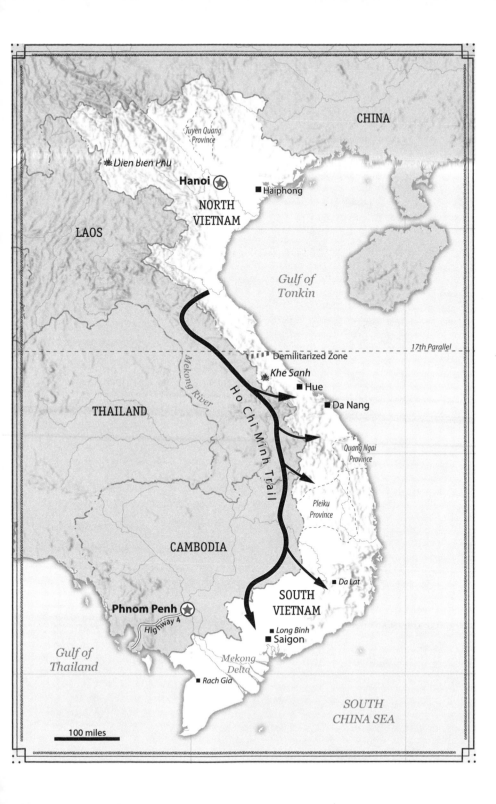

FOREWORD

THE ECHOES OF THE VIETNAM War are heard in these gripping accounts of women from around the world who were, in various ways, deeply and passionately involved with the war. These disparate voices span three decades, illuminating the feminine face of war and adding to the undeniable legacy of women's involvement in its perils. First, author Kathryn Atwood gives us an important lesson in Southeast Asian history, beginning with 1945. She provides a historical chronology of the Vietnam War while directing a spotlight on the bravery and achievements of not only the risk-taking women who participated in the war but also those who suffered gravely from its consequences. Their recollections paint pictures for us, unforgettable portraits.

For me, there is something different about this book. When I finished the last page, engrossed in the lives of these featured women, I contemplated why I felt awe and remorse. I was shaken. The author takes us on a journey back more than a half century to a time of unspeakable brutality, exemplary heroism, loss, and hope. It was a time when most women who had stepped up to serve humbly declared, like the French nurse Geneviève de Galard, serving in Vietnam in the 1950s, "I only did my duty." Under harrowing conditions with dying men all around her, she, the lone woman, dressed wounds and kept up morale in the face of mounting casualties. We read her story here and know she is an indisputable hero.

We read Dr. Dang Thuy Tram's diary entry about her patients: "Your blood has crimsoned our native land. . . . Your heart has stopped so that the heart of the nation can beat forever." Dr. Tram was dedicated to saving lives of the Communist guerrilla forces in underground hospitals very near to where my fellow nurses and I were saving lives of American soldiers in the 71st Evacuation Hospital, Pleiku, in 1969. She and I could not have been very far from each other. In her diary, she wrote of "hatred for the invaders." That was me! I was the invader. We were women on different sides of the war, yet we both were passionate about our work, we both loved our countries, we both loved our patients, and we both fought despair in watching young men suffer and die. She was killed in June 1970. She died for her country, a hero to her people; she was buried on her sacred ground. US military women (eight nurses) died in Vietnam too, their bodies shipped home. Each one a hero.

I was shaken because I was taken back to a time and place where my colleagues and I didn't know if the Vietnamese women working in our hospital wards were friend or foe. We did know they were stealing from us—our drugs, IV tubing and bottles, field dressings. They would do anything to save their husbands, brothers, fathers, and sons. Dr. Tram fought her war the same way I fought mine—ignoring the thuds of rockets and mortars landing around us, we saved lives the best we could with what we had. Only she was facing the stark terrors of the ravages of war in the country she loved, while I could fly home at the end of my tour.

I felt remorse in not taking the time to grasp or truly feel what it felt like for these women on the other side. That is not something we do when others are the enemy. We put distance between ourselves and them. Later, we look for understanding and reconciliation.

This book is not about proving the rightness or wrongness of the Vietnam War. This is a galvanizing chronicle of women who were caught up in the hellishness of war. Yet each of them found the spirit and stamina to overcome trauma and heartbreak with the endurance needed to survive and move forward. Some women drawn to the war chose their battles—US military nurses, civilian women in support of the US Armed Forces, civilian women from neighboring countries, journalists who brought the war's grim realities to the world's attention. These women who, despite naysayers proclaiming they didn't belong in a war zone, volunteered to serve in the jungles, rice paddies, and villages of Vietnam. Others had their battles chosen for them—children burned by napalm who faced a lifetime of recovery and political persecution in their own country; Vietnamese women furtively protecting their families, homes, and livelihood from destruction. We hear too from those on safer shores—the war protestors.

In revealing war's inhumanity, *Courageous Women of the Vietnam War* illuminates our shared humanity by bringing us these compelling voices from both sides of the conflict. We find their truths in their remembrances. Their inspiring stories deepen our understanding of war's exacting toll and leave us with remarkable insights into that turbulent era.

We need to look further, however, and see the personal cost for these daring women's devotion to duty. After years of suffering in silence, there is now a name, and treatment, for the lingering emotional trauma from war—post-traumatic stress disorder (PTSD). War may be as close to hell as we ever get, leaving nightmares, memories, and emotional wounds that require the healing powers of a lifetime. Sorrows can be borne if we unburden our stories. Yes, even for most of us who believe "I only did my duty."

—DIANE CARLSON EVANS

DIANE CARLSON EVANS was a captain in the US Army Nurse Corps from 1966 to 1972, serving in Vietnam in 1968 and 1969. Founder and president of the Vietnam Women's Memorial Foundation, she spearheaded a campaign to place in the nation's capital a national monument that recognized the contributions of military women to their country as well as civilian women's patriotic service. These efforts were rewarded when a bronze monument portraying three women and a wounded soldier was dedicated on November 11, 1993, at the Vietnam Veterans Memorial on the National Mall in Washington, DC.

INTRODUCTION

IN AD 40 TWO WOMEN, Trung Trac and Trung Nhi, did something that would make them legends in Vietnamese history: they led a military victory.

The Trung sisters, trained in the martial arts and witnesses to the brutal Chinese occupation of Vietnam, were inspired to lead a rebellion after Trac's husband was beheaded for attempting to do the same; the Chinese had hoped his execution would discourage further resistance.

It had the opposite effect, and a large band of Vietnamese rebel nobles, led by the Trung sisters, eventually captured 65 Chinese-controlled citadels. Trac was then crowned queen of a large territory.

She ruled only three years before the Chinese defeated her. Two hundred years later, Trieu Au, another Vietnamese woman, led an army of 1,000 men into battle against the Chinese. When asked why, she responded, "I want to rail against the wind and the tide, kill the whales in the sea, sweep the whole country to save the people from slavery, and I refuse to be abused." Her rebellion lasted only months before she too was defeated.

But her words and actions, along with those of the Trung sisters, passed into legend and would inspire generations of Vietnamese people to determinedly seek what these women had fought for: freedom.

Their centuries-long resistance against Chinese domination was eventually replaced by a struggle against the French. When a force of guerrilla fighters known as the Vietminh defeated the French in 1954, Vietnam, part of what the French called Indochina, was temporarily divided in two until nationwide elections could be held two years later. The First Indochina War was over.

But a new war began the following year. Instead of fighting the French, this time the Vietnamese people were fighting each other: the Communist North versus the allegedly democratic South. And the South had a powerful foreign champion: the United States, a nation that by the end of the First Indochina War had been vigorously supporting France against the Vietminh, footing 80 percent of France's war costs. The new war's official name was the Second Indochina War. Americans called it the Vietnam War. The Communist Vietnamese whom the Americans were trying to defeat on behalf of the South had a different name for the conflict: Khang Chien Chong My, or the Resistance War Against America. Most North Vietnamese just called it the American War.

These Communists considered the French and the Americans as having exactly the same goals—colonial oppression of their nation—and the two Indochina wars as being two halves of one whole. But the American War was not, as the previous conflict had been, an attempt to retain Vietnam as a wealth-producing colony. Rather, it was a disillusioning and ultimately tragic clash of cultures and ideals.

The United States was in Vietnam because of the Cold War. Communism—by then considered by the world's democracies to be just as dangerous as the Fascism they had defeated during World War II—was spreading throughout the world. It seemed to American leaders, and to those from the Far East democracies who joined them, that Vietnam was a key place to take a stand against this totalitarianism.

In their determination to stop the spread of Communism, however, these nations—the United States foremost among them—didn't take the time to thoroughly understand Vietnamese history and its people's way of thinking, nor did they allow themselves to admit that the South Vietnamese regime they were propping up as a buffer against the Communist North was in no way a democracy, as its leaders claimed. Rather, it was a brutal dictatorship that tortured and killed any of its own people whom it suspected of being Communists.

The culture clash between the Vietnamese South and North was a result of the French occupation. Those South Vietnamese who were educated, urban, and French speaking dearly hoped the Americans would save them from having to forfeit their comfortable lifestyle, which would surely happen under a totalitarian Communist government. For if the Americans couldn't save them, their own army certainly wouldn't: these wealthy Vietnamese, and the many corrupt officers of their Army of the Republic of Vietnam (ARVN) who had also largely rejected Eastern culture, did little to inspire their fellow Southerners with any sort of patriotism or motivation to fight.

Unlike the wealthy elite, the largest group of Southerners, the farmers, maintained traditional Eastern values, which taught them to respect whichever authority was in power.

But when their loyalty was simultaneously demanded by both sides—the Vietnamese Communists (Vietcong or VC) fighting secretly in the South and the ARVN soldiers working with the Americans—these farmers became snared in a war that brutalized their families and destroyed their simple way of life along with their precious ancestral lands.

US leaders hoped they could win a war of attrition; that is, they would cause so much loss and destruction as to make the Communists quit. The Americans measured success in body counts, the number of Communist fighters killed. But by making this their yardstick for success, Americans revealed a dangerous ignorance regarding the sincere and intense patriotism that made their enemies quite willing to risk their lives to see their country unified. So as the war progressed, Americans were increasingly baffled by this tiny nation's ability to endure and defy the world's greatest military power, year after destructive year.

Americans grew antagonistically divided over the war, and the US military draft became a lightning rod for that division. While fear drove some young men to either comply with their draft notices or flee the country, others on both sides of the issue were motivated by deeply held principles. But it was a rare individual who credited those with opposing viewpoints for acting on the courage of their convictions.

The very concept of patriotism was hotly debated in the United States during the war. Many in the widely diverse antiwar organizations were convinced they were serving their country by doing whatever they could to end its involvement in a war they believed pointless and immoral. On the other side were those who served in Vietnam out of an equally strong sense of patriotic duty that was often coupled with a desire to emulate the heroism of the World War II generation (which in many instances were their own parents).

Americans holding and implementing these conflicting points of view not only were at odds with each other but also often felt personally betrayed by those on the other side.

The United States did finally pull out of Vietnam, losing, in a sense, its own war of attrition. Within two years, North Vietnam had defeated the South, and the nation was united under the Communist flag. But the new regime was so oppressive—and its economy so depressed—that even many who had fought to unite the country now did all they could to flee it.

Although all memorials to dead ARVN soldiers were destroyed after the reunification, the new government tried to give meaning to the conflict by commemorating, in various ways, the 1.1 million Communist combatants who had been killed during the war. Americans, on the other hand, bitterly disillusioned with their government and the disastrous war, basically ignored their own 2.5 million Vietnam veterans for many years.

Finally, in 1982 the first part of the Vietnam Memorial was erected in Washington, DC, in remembrance of the 58,000 American Vietnam War veterans killed or missing in action. This initiated a nationwide acknowledgment of Vietnam veterans, but at that point, most of the attention focused on the war's male participants. Why? Perhaps because war is generally waged by men and considered to be their duty.

So when women volunteer to participate in a war, they exhibit a particular kind of courage, to face not only the dangers of battle but also the negative opinions—perhaps even their own—of those who don't believe them capable of enduring war's grueling difficulties.

The women whose stories are included in this book represent all sides of the Vietnam War: Northern and Southern Vietnamese; French, Americans, and Australians; military nurses

and a peace activist. Through their varied experiences, perhaps
we can gain insight into the many facets of this complex and
tragic conflict. And because most of these women—each representing thousands more with similar stories—voluntarily put
themselves in harm's way to make their contributions, they
deserve our respect. After all, the Trung sisters and Trieu Au
are revered not only for their courage in battle but also for being
in the battle at all.

Part I
1945–1956

HO CHI MINH'S REVOLUTION

★

ON SEPTEMBER 2, 1945, a 55-year-old Vietnamese man stood in Bao Dinh Square, Hanoi, before a crowd of 400,000 people. He was about to deliver a speech that would alter the course of history. He began with the following words: "All men are created equal. They are endowed by their Creator with certain inalienable rights. Among these are life, liberty, and the pursuit of happiness."

Who was this man, and why was he quoting the American Declaration of Independence? He called himself Ho Chi Minh, and he was attempting to bring about his own nation's independence.

That wouldn't be easy. During the 19th century, the French had struggled long and hard to make Vietnam their colony. Finally, in 1887, after a decisive military victory, they claimed it for their own. It was now, they said, part of an Indochinese Union that also included Cambodia (and, six years later, Laos).

They named southern Vietnam Cochin China, the central area Annam, and the northern region Tonkin. To further erode any sense of Vietnamese nationalism, they called all Vietnamese people Annamites.

The French built roads, railroads, and shipping ports in Vietnam, but they didn't pay for these projects themselves; they taxed the Vietnamese people. These taxes were so high many middle-income families could pay them only by selling their land, which had been in their families for generations. This was a tragedy on many levels. Most Vietnamese worshipped their ancestors, who were buried on their lands, and tending their graves was considered a sacred duty. And once landless, many families' survival often meant working on French-owned plantations for low wages and in brutal conditions.

Some Vietnamese people, however, fared well during the French occupation. The French conquered the South first, and when they did, Southern officials—the revered mandarins who were highly educated officials trained in the Chinese tradition—fled north. The French chose and trained new Vietnamese men for positions of authority. These new officials spoke, dressed, and thought like Frenchmen, and were completely dependent on their colonial overlords not only for their identities but for their often lavish incomes as well.

But the French found the rest of Vietnam much more difficult to conquer and, once in their control, more difficult to rule. This was especially true in the North, an area they had conquered last and where they had to constantly battle nationalistic movements, such as that led by Ho Chi Minh.

Born with the name Nguyen Sinh Cung (and later taking the name Nguyen Ai Quoc), the man who would come to embody Vietnamese nationalism began, in the early 1940s, to call himself Ho Chi Minh, meaning "he who has been enlightened." As a young man he had traveled to Paris, where he met other expatriate Vietnamese who were interested in setting their nation free from French colonization.

After spending some of the 1920s and 1930s with the Communist Party in China and the Soviet Union, Ho returned to Vietnam in 1941, during World War II, to lead a Communist force determined to win Vietnamese independence. This force was the Viet Nam Doc Lap Dong Minh (Vietnam Independence League), or Vietminh for short.

The Vietminh saw major growth during this time, perhaps in part because they then had an additional enemy to further spur their resistance: the Japanese, who since September 1940 had ruled Indochina through a puppet government led by Vietnamese emperor Bao Dai. In 1945 the Vietminh gained stronger support and became folk heroes among the Vietnamese when the Japanese—through their policies and seizure of crops—caused a national famine, killing approximately two million Vietnamese people, and the Vietminh robbed Japanese storehouses and gave grain to the people.

The Vietminh had powerful international allies as well. American intelligence agents of the Office of Strategic Services (OSS), seeking to undermine the Japanese, parachuted into Vietnam and provided the Vietminh with arms and training. The Vietminh, in turn, rescued downed US airmen and provided Americans with intelligence on the Japanese.

OSS agents were in the audience when Ho Chi Minh gave his powerful speech in Hanoi on September 2, 1945, declaring Vietnamese independence and the establishment of what he called the new Democratic Republic of Vietnam. On this same day, Japanese officials formally surrendered to the Allies in Tokyo Bay, thus officially ending World War II. The Vietminh had already forced Bao Dai to abdicate, and Ho was trying to fill the power vacuum before the French could return and reclaim their possessions. By peppering his speech with references to the US Declaration of Independence, Ho hoped to continue his alliance with the Americans and gain their support for his cause.

But at that very moment, US Merchant Marine ships transporting American servicemen home received orders to transport French soldiers to Vietnam. After nearly five years of a humiliating German occupation, France was determined to regain some national dignity by reclaiming its colonial possessions in the Far East. Assisting its wartime ally to accomplish this was more important to the United States than allowing another Far East nation to fall to Communism, the ideology that had become the new enemy to Western democracies.

If Ho's speech didn't inspire Americans in any significant way, it had a bracing effect on the Vietnamese people who heard it. Their idea of a government was always the "will of heaven"; that is, they believed they were destined to follow whoever was in charge. Up to that point, they'd believed French rule had been heaven's will for them. But when Ho mentioned that the French had not once but "twice sold our country to the Japanese," it seemed to most Vietnamese people standing there that the French were no longer conquerors to be feared and obeyed. Ho and the Vietminh were clearly destined to lead Vietnam.

The French didn't see things that way. On September 22, 1945, French paratroopers and legionnaires swarmed into Saigon, Cochin China's capital city. Despite the fighting that immediately broke out between the Vietnamese and the French, both soldiers and civilians, war was not Ho's aim. He tried to negotiate with the French. Negotiations broke down. He tried to gain support from US president Harry S. Truman. President Truman didn't answer Ho's communications. More fighting erupted between the Vietminh and the ever-increasing number of determined French soldiers who branched out from the South in their quest to regain complete control over Vietnam.

In February 1947 the French reached Hanoi. The Vietminh retreated into the jungles to wage a guerrilla-style war, destroying all other nationalist movements without Communist roots. Meanwhile, Ho sought to gain more followers by downplaying the Vietminh's Communist ideology. Instead he presented it as an organization solely dedicated to Vietnam's liberation. He changed the name of the Vietnamese Communist Party to Lao Dong, or the Worker's Party. Northern Vietnamese from all walks of life joined the Vietminh to support what they called the French War.

Ho convinced his followers that fighting the French for Vietnamese independence was a sacred duty that might take years. Then he held out for a long war, telling one French visitor, "You can kill ten of my men for every one I kill of yours. But even at those odds, you will lose and I will win."

By 1953 France was feeling the impact of those losses. Ninety thousand French soldiers of the Indochina War were dead, wounded, missing, or being held prisoner. And the end was nowhere in sight. The French people now referred to the Indochina War as *la sale guerre*, or "the dirty war." Despite heavy French losses, Ho still knew that for the French to negotiate on his terms, he would have to gain some sort of impressive victory.

In November 1953, in a small Vietnamese village called Dien Bien Phu located near the Laotian border, that victory looked surprisingly possible. The general in charge of the French forces in Indochina, Henri Navarre, ordered Dien Bien Phu occupied and held. The battle that followed would forever alter the course of Vietnamese history but would affect far more than Vietnam and France. Those on the outside would see it as a battle in the Cold War: Communist China and the Soviet Union were both supporting the Vietminh. The United States was supporting the French.

The day after the French surrendered to the Vietminh, representatives from several nations began the Geneva Conference, meeting to decide several issues, one of them a peaceful resolution to the Indochina conflict. Vietnam was divided into two military "regroupment zones." This temporary division was to be resolved in 1956 after a nationwide election. That election was never held.

The First Indochina War was over. The second would soon begin.

XUAN PHUONG

Young Revolutionary

XUAN PHUONG WAS BORN IN 1929 in Hue, a city in the central portion of Vietnam that the French called Annam, but she grew up farther south in Dalat. Her family was affluent, a direct result of its connection to the French government: her father was the supervisor of a French school.

When Phuong was in grade school, her uncle Hien came to live with her family. Phuong's parents warned her and her siblings to not mention his presence to anyone, and Phuong quickly discovered why: Uncle Hien constantly criticized the French. After one week's stay, Phuong's father sent Hien to work as overseer on the family's coffee plantation, 70 miles away. When Phuong went to visit during the summer, Uncle Hien showed her the crude shacks that housed the *mois*, the local plantation laborers. The French government, Hien explained, had given the plantation to Phuong's father with instructions to hire only *mois*, as they could be paid cheaply. The memory of a sick old *mois* man too weak to work but too poor to purchase necessary medicine would forever haunt Phuong.

In 1945 Phuong went to live with relatives in Hue in order
to attend high school. There she met her uncle Tay, another
relative with dangerous political views. He told her about the
Vietminh and their revolutionary aims for Vietnamese independence. And at her new school, called Khai Dinh for the father of
Vietnamese emperor Bao Dai, Phuong learned even more when
she was selected to join a club called the Association of Patriotic
Students, run by Vietminh recruiters. Here Phuong first heard
about someone named Nguyen Ai Quoc. She would later know
him as Ho Chi Minh.

Her teachers were divided along sharp political lines: two
were loyal to the Vietminh and three to the French. As enthusi-
asm for Vietnam's independence intensified, students who actually wanted to study were viewed with contempt by those who
were increasingly fascinated by the idea of revolution. Phuong
began to do resistance work for Uncle Tay, creating propaganda
leaflets and Vietnamese flags and carrying messages past Japanese sentries.

Toward the end of World War II, as the Allies were defeating
the Axis powers, the Japanese (part of the Axis) and the French
(part of the Allies) struggled for control of French Indochina. On
the night of March 9, 1945, Phuong was awakened by the sound
of gunfire. Her uncle burst into the house crying, "The Japanese
have disarmed the French!" He went off to join the Vietminh,
who sent Phuong and four other female students north to Hanoi
to study midwifery. The girls would never know exactly why
they had been chosen for this particular training, but they felt
honored to have been singled out.

In August Phuong and the other young midwife trainees
were told they must return home to Hue because the fighting
around Hanoi would soon become intense.

Back in Hue, on August 25, Phuong witnessed the public abdication of Bao Dai, the Vietnamese emperor who had been a puppet ruler during first the French and then the Japanese occupations. Emperor Bao Dai stood in front of his palace dressed in his ceremonial robes, surrounded by his weeping family and three Vietminh officials. A man's voice cried out, "From this day on, royalty is abolished in Vietnam."

Many in the audience cheered. Others wept. The emperor handed his royal seal and his ceremonial sword to one of the Vietminh officials, who waved both items in the air before placing them on a table. A cannon fired 21 times. The emperor's yellow flag was lowered and removed and the Vietminh flag raised in its place. The cannon fired again. Then the crowd ran into the royal palace and plundered it.

A short time later Phuong heard that the Allies had defeated the Japanese. Hue was overrun by representatives of the victors: bedraggled, emaciated Chinese soldiers from Generalissimo Chiang Kai-shek's armies. After they left, soldiers of another nationality appeared in Hue. They were French. And they clearly intended to stay.

Phuong desperately wanted to help drive out the French soldiers. She left home and joined a small cadre, a group of trainees, young men and women who, like her, were educated and French literate. Their base was a large hut in a remote area, and their mission, under the guidance and training of a Vietminh leader named Sung, was to create propaganda leaflets. They disguised themselves as vendors and carefully distributed the leaflets to French soldiers at the local market. Phuong's leaflets explained her background and motivations, why she and her comrades had left their comfortable lives to fight for their nation's independence.

One evening the young women in the cadre placed some straw and peppercorns under a window of a hotel that was housing French soldiers. When the women set fire to the straw, it produced an enormous amount of smoke. The young women yelled, "French soldiers, do you know for whom you are fighting?"

The soldiers answered, "It is for you, Mesdemoiselles!" Then they shot into the darkness, but the young women all escaped unharmed.

Later the cadre traveled from village to village putting on simple theatrical productions that they hoped would inspire locals to embrace the revolution and support its fighters with food and shelter. The young actors had very little food to eat and no money; they were each supplied with only one rice ball per day. They slept in temples or on untraveled railroad tracks.

Phuong grew weary of the difficult, nomadic way of life, so she was relieved when she was eventually allowed to stay in one place with a group of former Hue students who were making explosives. From Hue, in March 1948, she was ordered to join Vietnam's first national research institute on weaponry in the jungle near Mount Khe Khao, in the Bac Kan region. These 50 physicists and former students lived in a real house, the first Phuong had stayed in since leaving home. Still, her life remained difficult in many ways. For instance, the only available food—rice carried through long jungle treks to avoid French outposts—was often rotten by the time she and the others received it.

But they didn't mind. Fascinated by the research, the team enjoyed a strong camaraderie and was thrilled to be directly useful to the resistance. Phuong also began to gather and edit articles for the institute's newspaper, *Dong*, a Vietnamese word meaning "detonation."

In September the institute was given orders to resettle in the jungle, about 125 miles from Hanoi, in Tuyen Quang Province.

Because the new location was a populated area, local workers and volunteers joined the resistance workers, and the institute became more productive than ever before.

Five months later, on February 4, 1949, an accidental explosion ripped the hand off one of the workers. Phuong was deeply shaken. Hoang, the assistant director of the institute, found her alone after work hours. The two had long harbored secret romantic feelings for each other, and Hoang had come to tell Phuong he would soon be leaving for the war front. This news was too much for Phuong, and she burst into tears.

"Why are you crying?" Hoang asked.

Phuong told him that she was so upset by the accident that she had lost the will to remain in the resistance.

In response, Hoang proposed marriage, saying, "This way there will always be two of us to face it all."

Phuong agreed, and the two were married on February 28. Phuong became pregnant, but before their son was born, Hoang was ordered to China for officer training and suggested she stay with his sister. Phuong gave birth to her baby boy, then traveled through the jungle on foot to her sister-in-law's house. She was shocked when her in-laws treated her not as a relative but as a household slave, this while still expecting her to find employment outside the home. Phuong began to work at the Finance Service, the Vietminh's financial headquarters. Then she left her in-laws and went with her baby to live in a dormitory with other Finance Service workers.

Ho Chi Minh lived nearby, and one day in 1951, Phuong met him. His appearance surprised her. "Nothing we had heard about him corresponded to this man in his fifties who was nothing but skin and bones," she wrote later. "With piercing eyes and a small beard, he dressed in the way of ethnic minorities, with brown shirt and pants, and his famous sandals."

He was also very kind, pitying the workers for their lack of quality food and advising them on specific health issues, such how to avoid malaria, a common jungle disease. Phuong was impressed that their great leader was so concerned with the details of their well-being.

And he was about to lead them to victory.

In October 1952 Ho's top general, Vo Nguyen Giap, and Giap's troops were occupying a small village called Dien Bien Phu, located near the Laotian border. When the French pushed them out, General Giap realized that Dien Bien Phu would be an ideal spot for a final showdown with the French army: the French would be isolated and dependent on parachute drops, whereas the Vietminh could be constantly reinforced from behind.

The Battle of Dien Bien Phu offered the Vietnamese the exhilarating hope of independence from the French. Each evening, Finance Ministry workers excitedly assembled around a large map that depicted combat areas with red pins and French casualty numbers on labels. "The atmosphere was electric," Phuong later wrote of this time. The slogan heard and repeated everywhere was "We work one and all for Dien Bien Phu."

Vehicles heading to Dien Bien Phu passed by the Finance Ministry all hours of the day and night: people on bicycles carried their village's required allotment of rice to the front lines of battle while trucks rolled by loaded with weapons and ammunition. Journalists, writers, and musicians all raced there as well, and Phuong heard many moving stories of long-separated friends reuniting at the front.

Hoang returned from China and was allowed to see Phuong for one night before he too left for the front, where he had been ordered to lead an artillery battalion.

On May 7, 1954, Phuong was at a printing shop discussing *Dong*'s latest issue with the printer. A radio was playing.

Suddenly the broadcaster began to shout. The Vietminh had defeated the French!

Phuong rushed outside to join the crowds of cheering people.

After the victory, Hoang was redeployed, and the Finance Ministry moved out of the mountains to Hanoi. So with her toddler and a new infant son, Phuong walked from the mountain dormitory to the city. At one point she became completely overwhelmed with exhaustion and hunger. She went to a temple to pray for help but soon fell sound asleep. Two wealthy women who had come to the temple with a food offering took pity on her and gave the offering to her and her children. One of the women, Madame Tung Hien, had known Phuong's father and insisted that Phuong and her children come live in her large Hanoi home. Phuong gratefully accepted.

But when Hoang arrived in Hanoi, he refused to enter Madame Tung's home. "Why are you living at a bourgeois woman's house?" he demanded.

Phuong explained that she had viewed the unacceptable alternative allotted by the Finance Ministry: an extremely tiny room.

"Phuong," he replied, "why don't you behave like everybody else?"

It was pointless to argue, and Phuong relented. Soon she was living with her children in a room so dark it needed artificial lighting even during the day. They had no furniture, only two jute sacks on the floor. Because the war was over and people who, like her, had previously lived in the jungle were now in Hanoi, the city's population swelled dangerously. People filled the streets, waiting in lines for everything from use of a toilet to food and water.

Phuong rarely saw her husband. Hoang liked neither the stifling room nor the cries of his hungry children, so he spent most of his time in the army barracks, where there was nonetheless no more to eat than at home.

At work Phuong could see a new social class forming: Communist Party members received all the high-ranking jobs. They constantly harassed Phuong and other non-Communist employees about joining the party and eavesdropped on their conversations for any comments that might possibly be considered offensive to Communism.

Phuong began to have nightmares. "I never could have imagined that this time of peace would be so hard to bear," she wrote later.

The government took complete control of all private homes and businesses in the city before turning to the countryside to initiate what would be known as "land reform." To accomplish this, they trained small teams of educated people. Phuong's team included five physicians, two of whom had lived in the jungle during the war. The team members were trained by a Communist *doi*, or team leader. "You people have benefited from good living in the past, whereas . . . we have always been exploited," the *doi* began. "We are going to make you understand . . . why it is necessary to wipe out all landowners without the slightest pity."

After their training, the group traveled from village to village. They would stay with the poorest family and ask them to identify the wealthiest villagers. The neighbors of one man, the owner of five taxis, falsely accused him of being a landowner. When a young boy tried to blindfold him before his execution, the doomed man refused, saying, "No, I want to look at this slaughter up to the end." Just before he was shot, he said, "It's shameful. Down with Communism."

What have all these long years in the Resistance been sacrificed for? Phuong asked herself as she observed these grim proceedings. *What happened to our lofty ideals?*

When she returned to Hanoi, Phuong continued to hear the results of the land reform: each day's denunciations and executions were broadcast to the public via loudspeakers. She felt as if she were witnessing the utter destruction of a civilization.

The land reform didn't stop until the parents of a prominent Communist official were sentenced to death. Despite its supposed purpose of wealth distribution, the land reform's two-year reign of terror had done nothing to raise anyone's standard of living. Life was bleaker than ever for most.

Although they didn't have much more money than anyone else, top Communist Party members owned the most beautiful homes and were the only Vietnamese to own cars. This new social structure affected the military as well: Hoang was forced to leave the army, "for the good of the people," he was told. Officials had checked his background and determined that he was too bourgeois—middle class and materialistic. He spent all day and night lying down and staring at the ceiling in their tiny, airless room. Phuong feared he was becoming suicidal.

He eventually recovered some hope, and in 1963 Phuong was given a new job, at the Ministry of Foreign Affairs. Four years later, while working there, she was asked to assist a German filmmaker named Joris Ivens, a personal friend of Ho Chi Minh.

As she helped Joris film life at the 17th parallel (the dividing line between the North and South), an area the United States was now heavily bombing, Phuong grew to admire the astonishing resilience of the people who lived there. Noticing her interest, Joris suggested to Phuong that she also become a filmmaker. After repeated requests to the government over a period of several years, she began working in Vietnam's film industry and for more than a decade made documentary films for Vietnamese television.

Phuong, second from right, working on *17 Parallel—People's War* with filmmaker Joris Ivens, second from left, 1967. *Xuan Phuong*

By 1989, however, 60-year-old Phuong had grown restless. "I had spent my life depending on others," she wrote later of this time, adding, "I had sacrificed all that I had for the benefit of a collective society. I reasoned that the moment had finally come for me to live for myself."

The government allowed Phuong to travel to Paris and remain there for two years. And when she returned to Vietnam, she moved to Saigon, now renamed Ho Chi Minh City, where she was allowed to open an art gallery called the Lotus Gallery, which she still runs to this day.

LEARN MORE

Ao Dai: My War, My Country, My Vietnam by Xuan Phuong with
Danièle Mazingarbe (EMQUAD International, 2004).
The English translation of Phuong's originally French
memoir.

Lotus Gallery website, www.lotusgallery.com.vn.

"Nguyen Thi Xuan Phuong—Galerie Lotus," www.youtube.com
/watch?v=KFvPPC-_Kr4/.
French-language interview (no subtitles) with Xuan Phuong
in the Lotus Gallery.

GENEVIÈVE DE GALARD

"I Only Did My Duty"

AT 4:30 ON THE AFTERNOON of May 7, 1954, the valley of Dien Bien Phu in Northern Vietnam was eerily quiet. Only hours earlier it had been shaken by the deafening roar of cannons.

French officers and soldiers who had earlier destroyed the remaining ammunition at Dien Bien Phu's French garrison (military post) were now quietly drinking champagne, another valuable they didn't want to leave behind. While these men solemnly toasted each other good-bye, they waited for the approach of the Vietminh, a guerrilla force that had just shocked the world by defeating them.

Waiting nearby with her patients was a military nurse named Geneviève de Galard.

During the 1930s Geneviève attended a grade school named Cours Louise-de-Bettignies. She was profoundly impressed with her teacher's stories about the school's namesake, a brilliant French agent who had worked for British intelligence during World War I and had died while in German captivity.

Geneviève's own family had a long history of military service: one of her ancestors had fought with the famous medieval hero Joan of Arc. Her late father and uncles had been French army officers, and many of her male relatives had fought in World War I.

So it was hardly surprising when, in January 1953, 27-year-old Geneviève joined the military herself, becoming a flight nurse with the Groupement des Moyens Militaires Transports Aériens, or GMMTA, the air transport service of the French air force. The GMMTA evacuation planes flew to the areas where the French military was at war—Algeria and Indochina—and transported the French wounded to Saigon and Paris.

In late 1953 the French army—and the evacuation nurses who supported them—increasingly focused on a remote camp in Indochina situated near a small village named Dien Bien Phu. The commander of the French army in Indochina, General Henri Navarre, decided that it would be an ideal spot to place a garrison of soldiers, who could protect Laos, cut Vietminh supply lines in the area, and prepare for a battle he was sure the French would win. Although Dien Bien Phu was surrounded by jungle and could only be accessed by air, French soldiers were improving its airfield and readying it for use.

On January 12, 1954, Geneviève landed there for the first time to pick up a planeload of wounded men. The camp was preparing for war, as she described later:

> From the air it was a universe of tunnels, trenches, and shelters whose entrances were revealed and reinforced by logs and sandbags. Machine-gun posts were spotted on the hillsides, and on the plain, and as we descended to land, I could see the brown tarps that still covered the shelters. Once I landed, the hills, green and wooded

seemed suddenly less hostile than the vast jungle universe we had flown over with its menacing density. In the distance a few rice fields still quivered in the wind, but the camp was closed in by a threatening jungle where paths must be carved out by machete.

Geneviève at Dien Bien Phu in February 1954, wearing her flight evacuation uniform. *Geneviève de Heaulme*

The Vietminh, who had been creating diversions elsewhere while quietly digging artillery trenches and tunnels as close as possible around Dien Bien Phu, launched their first major attack on the French garrison on March 13, 1954.

Geneviève arrived in Dien Bien Phu once again, on March 28 at 5:45 AM. The morning fog was so thick her pilot couldn't see where to land. His third attempt was successful except that he ran the plane into some barbed wire. The oil radiator was punctured, and the plane wouldn't be operational until repaired.

But it would never be used again: after the passengers had disembarked and as the fog lifted, the plane became visible to the Vietminh, who took aim and fired. Geneviève watched it go up in flames.

With the plane destroyed, she had to wait for a return flight and spent the night in Dien Bien Phu. Meanwhile, soldiers eager to get in touch with their families, deluged her with personal letters to deliver for them.

The next morning, while waiting for the arrival of an evening plane that would evacuate her and 250 desperately wounded men, Geneviève distributed items the Red Cross was parachuting into the camp: cigarettes, milk, and oranges. As day wore into night, one Vietminh shell after another exploded on the landing field.

By midnight, rain was pouring out of an ink-black sky, and the damaged landing field was thick with slippery mud. The wounded were carried out to meet the plane. Geneviève's jeep became stuck in the mud. As she sloshed her way to the landing spot on foot, she saw a plane approaching. She didn't think it would be able to land safely. Apparently someone in the control tower shared her opinion, because, rather than landing, the plane kept going.

Geneviève and the wounded returned to the garrison.

The following afternoon, at 4:00, a new Vietminh attack began, this one with Soviet-made howitzer cannons. "I felt as if it was the end of the world," wrote Geneviève later. "The impacts shook our bunker. Pieces of earth fell from the roof. . . . Nobody said a word. All around there were wounded men bearing their sufferings with courage, and I knew that at dawn, when the battle decreased, the stretcher bearers would bring the new wounded. How could I sleep?"

She couldn't. "The shelling lasted all night," she wrote. "The din was terrifying."

When the shelling stopped, it was clear that Geneviève would be staying indefinitely at Dien Bien Phu. The Vietminh had moved closer to the garrison, rendering the landing field impossible to use. Geneviève wrote later that although the high command didn't want women at Dien Bien Phu, and although she was a flight nurse, not a ground medic, there was only one thing she could now do: "care for and stay with the wounded."

Major Paul Grauwin, MD, was the surgeon in charge of Dien Bien Phu's main 44-bed underground hospital. He put Geneviève to work there. While the two surgeons "performed miracles," Geneviève gave shots, changed bandages, and distributed medicine by the light of an electric lamp.

Because the wounded were no longer being evacuated, the main hospital became overwhelmed with wounded men. Hundreds were also placed elsewhere throughout the camp, including battalion dressing stations and hastily dug shelters. Geneviève made a point to visit everyone she could, distributing Red Cross items and checking on the wounded soldiers' progress.

Dr. Grauwin was very nervous about Geneviève leaving the main hospital, and he had reason to be: there was danger not only from Vietminh artillery assaults but also from the continuous rains. Mud was everywhere: the tunnels, the shelters, the lower-level beds. Once, while outside, Geneviève sunk hip-deep into the mud and had to be pulled out by two medics. The humidity also brought a proliferation of biting insects, which afflicted everyone, especially the men wearing casts, who were already in agony with humidity-induced skin irritation.

It seemed like conditions in Dien Bien Phu could not get much worse for the French. But they did. On April 3 the Vietminh announced a half-hour cease-fire so that both sides could remove their wounded from the battlefield. When the French soldiers walked toward the enemy lines, however, they made a horrible discovery: the Frenchmen they found on the stretchers were not wounded; they were dead, their bodies mutilated. Morale sunk even lower among the French troops.

Yet as the enemy moved in, Geneviève's very presence lightened the profound sense of hopelessness falling upon the garrison. Later that day a large group of French paratroopers landed in the area. One of them, when he saw Geneviève, exclaimed cheerfully, "What do you know? There's a woman here!"

Though overwhelmed with medical work, Geneviève tried to attend to the men's emotional needs as well, explaining later that "when wounded, the toughest man becomes as vulnerable as a child and needs to feel supported. . . . In Dien Bien Phu I was, in a way, a mother, a sister, a friend."

One man whose legs were paralyzed told Geneviève, "Every time you walk into my room my morale goes up 100 percent." So Geneviève visited him every day, praising him as he tried to wiggle his toes.

As the battle raged, Lieutenant Colonel Pierre Langlais, whom Geneviève considered to be "the soul and mind of the defense of Dien Bien Phu," sent her a message: A large American press agency in Hanoi, representing the famous American war correspondent Marguerite Higgins, wanted to help Geneviève write her memoirs. They would pay her well.

Geneviève laughed, returned to her work, and never responded to what she termed "that astonishing offer."

On April 29 Geneviève received two offers she did accept: a Legion of Honor and a Cross of War from Lieutenant Colonel Langlais. He had found the Cross of War in the camp, and the Legion of Honor had actually been intended for him. (The one intended for Geneviève had accidentally landed in enemy territory.)

Lieutenant Colonel Langlais wrote Geneviève's awards citation, which read: "Geneviève has earned the admiration of everyone for her quiet and smiling dedication. . . . With unmatched professional competence and an undefeatable morale, she has been a precious auxiliary to the surgeons and contributed to saving many human lives."

Geneviève particularly loved the last phrase: "She will always be, for the combatants at Dien Bien Phu, the purest incarnation of the heroic virtues of the French nurse."

On the morning of May 6 Geneviève heard a "terrifying noise . . . a sort of howl followed by an explosion." She heard one of the men say, "That is Stalin playing the organ" (referring to the sound of Soviet-made rocket launchers nicknamed "Stalin's organs").

All night long the battle raged. "A counterattack succeeded," Geneviève wrote later, "raising again a high wave of hope. One position was regained. Everyone sensed that the night would be decisive. . . . The French artillery, lacking ammunition, had almost stopped firing while Stalin's organs fired in relays and increased by tenfold the power of the Vietminh artillery."

"The battle was now so intense that the injured could no longer reach our unit and had to wait where they fell until the usual lull at dawn," she described.

Geneviève went to Lieutenant Colonel Langlais's command post to hear the latest news of the battle so she could relate it to her patients: "I shared with the combatants moments of high hopes, when a position was retaken by our men, and the awful moments, during the heartbreaking adieux of the unit commanders: 'The Viets are thirty feet away. Give our love to our families. It is over for us.' My heart tightened as though I were hearing the last words of the condemned."

"By dawn, all hope had disappeared," she wrote later. Some of the officers considered breaking through enemy lines that evening in the direction of Laos. But they abandoned the idea. None of the remaining combatants were strong enough to do anything of the kind. Geneviève wrote, "The fighting would cease to avoid the massacre of the wounded."

She was told that the cease-fire would begin at 5:00 PM, May 7. Around 4:30, as she said good-bye to the officers, she saw that they "were all close to tears." As one captain shared champagne with the men and Geneviève distributed last cigarettes, she noticed that a "strange silence settled over the valley."

At 5:30 the Vietminh arrived. They ordered everyone out of the medical unit, even the stretcher cases. Geneviève was horrified by what she saw outside: dead bodies everywhere. The Vietminh ordered the able-bodied medics and wounded to march forward. As they did, their path crossed with "columns of French prisoners marching northwards, their shoulders hunched and their eyes filled with sorrow."

The Vietminh camp commandant summoned Geneviève for an interview. He commended her for her work and praised his leader, Ho Chi Minh. Geneviève felt he was playing some sort of mind game with her, one she didn't understand. She kept

//

THE POWs OF DIEN BIEN PHU

Immediately following the French defeat at Dien Bien Phu, approximately 9,000 French POWs began their march to the Vietminh POW camps, one of them 300 miles away, the other 450. The men marched 12 miles per day for approximately one to two months. Most who began the march with battle wounds died quickly; a multitude of others succumbed to jungle diseases or dysentery from drinking unclean water. Some men attempted to escape but seldom with long-term success—any villagers they would have had to ask for assistance considered them the hated enemy. When the survivors arrived at the camps, they were met by thousands of other French POWs struggling to survive in shockingly rudimentary conditions. While the captives were not subjected to physical torture, if they didn't fully cooperate with the daily enforced Communist indoctrination, their small rations were withheld.

The POWs were finally released between August and October 1954. Even those who had been in captivity only since May—that is, 3,900 of the original 9,000 veterans of the Dien Bien Phu surrender who had survived the march and imprisonment—were skeletal. They came home to a French public disgusted by the war and its representatives. Like the Americans who would follow them, these veterans were advised to wear civilian clothing to avoid attacks from their fellow citizens. Many suffered with substance abuse and relationship problems after returning home; some even took their own lives.

//

repeating, "Since you speak of the humanity and clemency of your president, the only humanitarian solution would be to authorize the evacuation of the wounded."

On May 19 the Vietminh allowed a group of wounded men to be evacuated in honor of Ho Chi Minh's birthday. Two days later, they told Geneviève she must leave as well. She refused. Up to this point, the Vietminh had allowed her to nurse her patients with what medical supplies they hadn't taken from her, and she couldn't bear the thought of leaving them. But more to the point, she didn't want to take up the space of a wounded man in an evacuation plane.

Three days later, however, the Vietminh would not take no for an answer; the international presses were implying that they were holding Geneviève at Dien Bien Phu against her will.

When Geneviève disembarked from the first flight of her trip home to France, in Luang Prabang, the capital of Laos, a group of legionnaires honored her with a formal presentation of arms.

It was night by the time she reached Hanoi. When the plane door opened, Geneviève was temporarily blinded by the flash of cameras. She was big news. The press conference that followed the next morning boiled down to two basic questions: "Were you scared?" and "Were you afraid to die?" Because she was deeply religious, Geneviève said she didn't fear death. But she did admit to being afraid once: during her initial interview with the Vietminh.

When she arrived in Paris a short time later, she was hounded by the French press and offered money if she would agree to have her story made into a film. She refused the offer and did her best to avoid the press, instead busying herself with what she considered important work: corresponding with the families of men who had been at Dien Bien Phu and who were now prisoners of war. To accomplish this task, she took one month's leave of absence from the French air force. Although she tried to remember everyone she had met at Dien Bien Phu, she often didn't recognize them from the photos their families

Geneviève in Luang Prabang, in the paratrooper uniform she wore while staying at Dien Bien Phu, on the cover of the magazine *Paris Match*. *Paris Match*

sent; the clean men in these photos looked so different from her unshaved patients.

Two months later, on July 26, 1954, Geneviève was in New York City being honored with a ticker tape parade. US president Dwight D. Eisenhower had invited her there and awarded her with the Presidential Medal of Freedom. Geneviève had felt overwhelmed by the invitation itself but didn't think she could refuse; this was the first time since 1821 that a foreigner had been invited by an act of Congress to the United States on an official visit.

During the exhausting three-week tour that followed, the American press began to call Geneviève the "Angel of Dien Bien Phu." Whenever she was asked to speak, she said something along the following lines: "I haven't earned this honor, because I only did my duty. . . . My thoughts, at this moment are with all those who are still over there and who, far more than I, have earned this honor that you offer."

Geneviève returned to Paris, but when her contract with the French air force expired on July 15, 1955, she decided to go back to New York for training at a rehabilitation center there. Then she returned to Paris and put her new skills to work, helping survivors of Dien Bien Phu who were learning to live with prosthetic limbs.

In 1956 Geneviève married Captain Jean de Heaulme, whom she met while in Indochina (but who had not been at Dien Bien Phu).

Decades later, they returned to Vietnam, but Geneviève couldn't bear to visit Dien Bien Phu. During this trip, she encountered more Vietnamese people than she had during the war. Though she could not respect Vietnam's government, she did greatly admire its people, who, she said, "have suffered so much throughout their history and manifest their attachment to the land . . . and who want to show to all the nations a . . . civilization of their own."

Geneviève and Jean had three children and three grandchildren and today live in Paris, where Geneviève still receives communications—via letter and in person—from veterans of the battle and others interested in her wartime experiences. She is also regularly invited to attend official military ceremonies.

The de Heaulmes are members of Vietnam Esperance, an organization designed to help Vietnamese Catholics and that built a chapel for them near Dien Bien Phu. The organization recently received permission from the Vietnamese government to build a church in the center of the village.

In 2003 Geneviève wrote her memoir, and it was translated into English in 2010.

LEARN MORE

The Angel of Dien Bien Phu: The Sole French Woman at the Decisive Battle in Vietnam by Geneviève de Galard (Naval Institute Press, 2010).

"Geneviève de Galard: The Angel of Dien Bien Phu," www.you tube.com/watch?v=3HK3Zeeg3wA.
French-language video testimony by Geneviève, with subtitles and images.

Hell in a Very Small Place: The Siege of Dien Bien Phu by Bernard B. Fall (Harper Collins, 1966).

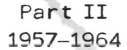

Part II
1957–1964

NGO DINH DIEM'S CIVIL WAR

★

ONE MAN'S DECISION WAS largely to blame for turning the First Indochina War into the second. The man was Ngo Dinh Diem. His momentous decision? Refusing to allow his people to vote in the 1956 national election.

Formerly Bao Dai's prime minister, Diem had been able to declare himself president of the new Republic of Vietnam on October 26, 1955, only because he'd rigged an election in his favor. But because a national election would be impossible to rig—he wouldn't be able to manipulate votes in the north—and because it was clear that Ho Chi Minh, the other candidate, would beat him in a landslide, Diem decided to prevent the South from participating in the election. He knew there were many Vietminh in the South waiting for the opportunity to fight for a unified Vietnam. So while Ho Chi Minh's government was conducting its land reform—murdering Northerners who were deemed disloyal to the Communist cause—Ngo Dinh Diem's government was doing the same in the South, killing anyone suspected of being loyal to the Vietminh.

To accomplish this, Diem passed laws allowing suspects to be tried and executed by a military tribunal without any access to appeals. Military personnel roamed the countryside on the lookout for suspects, who, when found guilty, were executed immediately and publicly, often in gruesome ways.

These laws and actions were harrowingly successful. By 1956 Diem's government had destroyed 90 percent of all Vietminh networks in the South. But this success was laced with failure; the Diem government's brutality drove many Southerners who would not have otherwise joined the Vietminh into their ranks.

Although the Vietminh in the South were eager to fight, Ho's government in Hanoi cautioned patience; perhaps Diem would soon self-destruct. But Diem wasn't going anywhere. The United States was propping him up. By the late 1950s there were 1,500 US military personnel in South Vietnam—officers, soldiers, helicopter pilots—whom Diem's government referred to as "advisors."

Ho's government in Hanoi decided it was time for serious action. In 1960 he created the National Liberation Front (NLF). The NLF's purpose was to overthrow the Southern government, then unify the nation, and it had its own army, called the People's Liberation Armed Forces (PLAF). But as early as 1956, both the US Information Services in Vietnam and Saigon newspapers referred to all Vietnamese fighting against the Diem regime as the Vietcong (VC), which was short for Viet Nam Cong San, or Vietnamese Communist. This name distinguished them from the Vietminh, the guerrilla force that had gained the profound respect of many Vietnamese people during the First Indochina War.

The VC worked tirelessly to overthrow the Southern government. They employed guerrilla warfare tactics against the

Southern government soldiers—the Army of the Republic of Vietnam (ARVN)—and the Americans and also sought to win the hearts and minds of the Southern people.

One way in which Diem tried to counteract the increasing influence of the VC in South and South-Central Vietnam was the construction of "agrovilles." This system forced farmers off their ancestral lands and into newly built villages where they could be watched and guarded, often while their former land was destroyed to keep the VC from using it. By 1961 the effort was renamed the Strategic Hamlet Program.

It was an utter failure. The people within the villages' gates were kept away from VC influence, yes, but at the cost of every-thing most precious to them. Diem failed to understand that for an enormous percentage of Vietnamese people, land repre-sented a historic and sacred sense of duty, family, and religion; most worshipped their ancestors, who were buried on their land.

Plus, the money that was supposed to support the people within the agrovilles usually found its way into the pockets of corrupt government officials. The subsequent shortages caused illness, starvation, and death in the villages, and those inside increasingly viewed the agrovilles as prisons. The failed Stra-tegic Hamlet Program, along with the general brutality of the Diem regime and its enormously high taxes, was directly responsible for sending even more South Vietnamese directly into the ranks of the VC.

The United States had initially hoped to tutor Diem in the ways of building a democracy but realized too late that he had his own ideas about how to run his country. Americans grew impatient with his corruption and ineptitude, especially when, on June 11, 1963, an elderly Buddhist monk burned himself to death on a busy Saigon intersection in protest of the Catholic

Vietnamese president's anti-Buddhist laws, which had been in place since the French occupation.

When the horrifying image of the burning monk hit the international presses and more just like it followed in the ensuing weeks, the entire world—including US president John F. Kennedy—asked what had driven all these monks to commit gruesome public suicides.

Throughout the rest of the summer, as the Diem regime cracked down on continued Buddhist protests (and as Diem's infamous sister-in-law, Madame Ngo Dinh Nhu, publicly referred to the monk burnings as "barbeques," offering to provide matches and gasoline for more), embarrassed US officials pleaded with Diem to listen to the complaints of the Buddhist community. Barricaded within his opulent presidential palace, Diem refused.

The Kennedy administration was through with him and secretly supported a coup that on November 1, 1963, ousted Diem and his brother, Ngo Dinh Nhu, from power. The brothers were killed in the coup, although President Kennedy had personally requested that their lives be spared.

The United States hoped that Diem's successor would be someone its government could enthusiastically support. He wasn't, nor were his successors as coup endlessly followed coup. The Southern government seemed hopelessly incapable of maintaining a regime stable enough to stand up to the VC. Perhaps it was time for the Americans to give up, go home, and allow the inevitable to happen.

They weren't about to do that, especially when Lyndon B. Johnson became the US president after the assassination of President Kennedy on November 22, 1963, just three weeks after Diem's execution. The following year was an election season wherein President Johnson would run against Senator Barry

Goldwater, a staunch anti-Communist. President Johnson, like most American politicians at the time, dreaded to be seen as anything less than a declared enemy of Communism and its international spread.

Johnson certainly didn't want his presidential legacy to be the Vietnam War. Instead he hoped to be remembered for his Great Society, a series of laws expanding the welfare state and designed to end poverty and racial injustice. But in his determination not to lose the Vietnam War, he became responsible for escalating it. If the Southern government couldn't stand on its own, he would "Americanize" the war; that is, he would increase US involvement.

His opportunity came on August 2, 1964, when he was told that North Vietnamese torpedo boats had fired on the USS *Maddox* in international waters in the northern Gulf of Tonkin. It is now widely and seriously doubted that any Vietnamese shots were fired, but at the time, the US Congress had no doubts; in a nearly unanimous vote, it passed the Gulf of Tonkin Resolution, which gave President Johnson the power to wage war without actually declaring it.

The Americanization of the Vietnam War was about to begin.

LE LY HAYSLIP

"Freedom Is Never a Gift"

PHUNG THI LE LY'S CLEAREST and earliest memories were of war. One day she and one of her older sisters, Lan, were playing together in the street near their home in Ky La, a village in central Vietnam, when the ground began to shake. All around them screaming villagers ran for cover. Lan grabbed Le Ly and pulled her into a trench by the side of the road and nervously sang:

French come, French come,
Cannon shells land, go hide!
Cannon shells sing,
Like a song all day!

French soldiers occasionally strolled into Ky La, but "even the friendly ones made us sick with horror," Le Ly wrote later. Part of this was simply due to their differentness: a tall man with Caucasian features seemed terrifying to an Asian child.

The French soldiers were also frightening because they weren't always so friendly. They knew that many villagers—including Le Ly's family—were helping the Vietminh and so, to keep them from doing this, French soldiers destroyed village after village. Once, when the French were rumored to be on their way to Ky La, Phung Van Trong, Le Ly's father, sent his family away to safety. Trong stayed behind and waited for days in a nearby river, knowing that if he was found, he would be accused of being a Vietminh. From a safe distance, he watched the French destroy the village. After they left, he managed to salvage enough furniture and tools to start over.

Trong's land—and his freedom—meant everything to him. One day, when Le Ly's five older siblings had moved out and her mother, Tran Thi Huyen, was gone for the day, Trong took his youngest daughter to the top of a hill behind the house where they could see the land all around the village. He told her about the cruel Chinese and French occupations.

"Freedom is never a gift," he said to Le Ly. "It must be won and won again."

Le Ly thought he was telling her to become a soldier. Trong laughed. No, he said; her job was to stay alive, help keep the village safe, and care for their large parcel of land so they—like everyone else in Ky La—could continue to grow rice. Then she would have children of her own who could pass on the family stories and tend the shrine of their ancestors. "Do these things well, Bay Ly," he said, calling her by the name her family members used, "and you will be worth more than any soldier who ever took up a sword."

But take up a sword she did, at least in play. In 1960, 10-year-old Le Ly and her village friends would often pretend to fight each other in war games. The French were long gone by this time. The new war participants were the Vietcong (VC)—the

Communist soldiers secretly fighting in the South—and the soldiers of the Army of the Republic of Vietnam (ARVN)—the soldiers of President Ngo Din Diem's Southern government. Most
of the children wanted to play VCs, even though they weren't
sure at that point if they'd seen one. Le Ly was uncomfortable
playing either side: her brother Bon Nghe had gone north in
1954 to join the Vietminh. But her sister Ba, who lived in the
nearby city of Da Nang, had married a policeman named Chin
who worked for Diem's government.

The village teacher, Manh, tried to turn his students' interest—and loyalties—to the Republic of Vietnam. He taught the
children songs praising the government and helped them put on
plays in which children playing President Diem and his sister-
in-law, Madame Ngo Dinh Nhu, always rewarded those who
defeated the VC.

Manh would pay the ultimate price for his political views.
One evening Le Ly glanced out the window and saw a group of
strange men in black clothing rush into Manh's house. When
the strangers came out, one of them was holding a gun to the
teacher's head. They forced him to walk to the road. Le Ly could
no longer see them, but she heard Manh begging for his life.
Two gunshots silenced him.

The strangers ran a new flag up the schoolhouse flagpole.
Their leader, shouting in an accent that sounded odd to Le Ly's
ears, said, "Your children need their education but *we* will teach
them." Anyone who dared touch the new flag, he threatened,
would be shot like Manh, "that traitor."

The VC had come to Ky La.

ARVN soldiers arrived the next day, pulled down the VC flag,
and gave the villagers materials with which to build a defensive perimeter—barbed wire, steel girders, cement. The villagers were directed to dig trenches and build watchtowers from

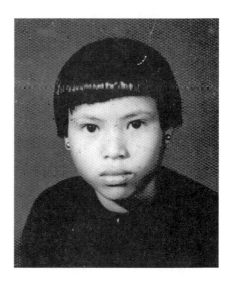

Le Ly, age 12.
Le Ly Hayslip

bamboo. Then the soldiers set up ambushes around the village and told the villagers to hide indoors. After waiting and watching for a few days, the ARVN soldiers left.

The VC returned immediately. They destroyed the defensive perimeter. "We are the soldiers of liberation," their leader said to the assembled villagers. "Ky La is our village now—and yours."

Which side would win the loyalty of Ky La?

The villagers were somewhat inclined to follow the VC since many of their young men had already gone north. And after arresting, imprisoning, beating, and shooting too many Ky La villagers for suspected VC activity, the ARVN soldiers lost whatever possible allegiance they may have hoped to inspire.

The VC, however, left nothing to chance. While the Ky La adults dug tunnels and bunkers under their homes so that the VC would be able to hide when necessary, the VC gathered the children for instruction. A new enemy, they told the children, had come to Vietnam: the Americans. Just like the French before them, the instructors said, President Diem's new allies were determined to enslave them.

Le Ly soon came face to face with this new enemy. One day, while caring for the family's water buffalo, she heard a sudden deafening roar. It grew so loud that the normally lazy animal trotted to the trees to hide.

In the sky, she saw two flying ships "whining and flapping like furious birds." The wind from these ships blew off her sunhat. She fell to her knees. She thought she was going to die. Then she raised her eyes. The ship landed. "The dull green door on the side of the ship slid open, and the most splendid man I had ever seen stepped out onto the marshy ground," she wrote later.

He was enormously tall and fair skinned. "Still cowering, I watched his brawny, blond-haired hands raise binoculars to his eyes," she wrote. "He scanned the tree line around Ky La, ignoring me completely." After saying something in a strange language to another man inside the ship, he went back inside.

"Instantly, the *flap-flap-flap* and siren howl increased and the typhoon rose again," Le Ly described. "As if plucked by the hand of god, the enormous green machine tiptoed on its skids and swooped away, climbing steadily toward the treetops."

The next sound she heard was her father's voice.

"Bay Ly—are you all right?"

"The *may bay chuong-chuong*—the dragonflies—weren't they wonderful!" said Le Ly.

Her father scolded her, telling her that she had just seen Americans. But by suppertime, he was no longer angry. In fact, he couldn't stop smiling.

Le Ly's mother, Huyen, still terrified by the event, angrily asked her husband to explain his smiling face.

The whole village was talking about Le Ly's courage, Trong said: she had stood her ground in the presence of the enemy. Le Ly didn't want to admit that it had been awe, not courage, that kept her from running away. Later she learned that standing still might have saved her life: villagers who ran from American or ARVN soldiers were often shot down for being suspected of VC activity.

The number of Americans in Ky La increased. They tried to win the villagers' loyalty with food and cigarettes and by caring for wounded civilians at American hospitals. They were also willing to go to great lengths to keep Ky La out of VC control. Americans and ARVN soldiers continuously searched the village for VC hideouts. When they suspected any house of being in the service of the VC, it was burned and the family taken away for questioning. Soon a large portion of Ky La had been destroyed.

This did nothing to deter the VC's fierce determination to retain their control over what and who remained. "After a while, our fear of the Viet Cong . . . was almost as strong as our fear of the [ARVN soldiers]," Le Ly wrote later. "If the [ARVN soldiers] were like elephants trampling our village, the VC were like snakes who came at us in the night."

Part of the way the VC asserted their control over the village was by forcing each villager to take on a specific task. When Le Ly turned 14, her job became sentry duty. She was to stand outside the village keeping watch for ARVN soldiers. If she saw any, she was to walk to a point in front of the village and give a silent signal to another sentry.

While at her post one February morning the following year, a heavy fog limited her vision. She gradually became aware of an odd noise off in the distance. Suddenly, out of the fog marched a large group of ARVN soldiers headed straight for Ky La. Le Ly was now between them and the village.

Terrified though she was, Le Ly realized what she must do: walk along the road in as casual a manner as possible, in front of the soldiers, to the signal point. She carried a bucket while on duty, as a prop. She now used it to collect the occasional potato or berry growing near the road.

Some of the soldiers glanced at her, but none of them stopped to question her. She finally reached the signal point. It was time to relay her message.

While on sentry duty, Le Ly wore three shirts. The outer, brown shirt indicated safety. The second was white and signaled potential danger.

The third shirt was black. It indicated a serious and present threat. Le Ly removed her top two shirts, then resumed picking berries.

She saw a woman approach, carrying a shoulder pole with a bucket on each end. The woman was also a VC sentry. She took one look at Le Ly, put down her buckets, turned around, and rushed away.

Le Ly walked home as quickly as possible, while still in view of the ARVN soldiers, and immediately changed her shirt.

When the soldiers swept the area and found no VC, they suspected that the berry-picking girl they'd noticed on the road might have given away their position. They rounded up several village girls of Le Ly's approximate age and height, Le Ly included. They blindfolded them, tied their hands behind their backs, then put them on a truck headed for Don Thi Tran prison a few miles away.

Le Ly's brother-in-law, Chin, personally vouched for her innocence, and she was released.

Back home, Le Ly discovered that the VC had made her a hero and written a song in her honor. They told her to learn it so she could teach it to the village children.

A few days later, holding the song sheet in her hand while resting in a hammock outside the village, she was approached by a group of linh biet dong quan—South Vietnamese Rangers, highly trained special forces who had stealthily entered the area.

One of them grabbed Le Ly by the collar. The song sheet fluttered to the ground. She prayed he wouldn't see it. But another ranger did. He showed it to the first ranger, who looked at it closely.

"Where did you get this, girl?" he demanded.

Le Ly stammered that she had found it blowing around in the wind. The ranger burned it in front of her, then ordered her hands tied behind her back before he took her to the village. As they walked, she saw other rangers skillfully darting in and out of the bushes and trees.

But shortly after they arrived in Ky La, the rangers went to help local ARVN soldiers battle some VC. When they returned weeks later, the ranger who had burned Le Ly's song sheet recognized her.

"Didn't we arrest you on the road a few weeks ago?" he asked.

Terrified, Le Ly tried to deny it.

"Yes," he said, ignoring her, "you're the girl with the filthy VC songbook."

The rangers drove Le Ly and another girl to My Thi, a military-run maximum-security prison outside the large city of Da Nang.

Le Ly was tortured horribly for three days. Then, without explanation, she was released. Her mother was waiting for her at her sister Ba's house. Huyen told Le Ly that she had used half of her dowry money to bribe an official.

No one had ever returned from My Thi so soon, and the VC in Ky La immediately suspected Le Ly of collaboration with the Southern government. One evening two young VC men took her to a thatched cottage. There a group of 20 VC sentenced her to death. The two young men took her to a freshly dug grave. Le Ly tried to prepare herself for death.

But instead of shooting her, the men raped her. Le Ly was devastated by the traumatic experience, and worst of all, she now worried that no good man would want to marry her, even though she had been sexually violated against her will. And if she didn't marry, how could she have children and continue her family's traditions?

The VC men who had raped her would not return her to Ky La, or it would be clear that they had not carried out her death sentence. Instead they took Le Ly to her relatives in a different village and, without explanation, told them she must stay with them.

After her parents discovered where she was, her mother, Huyen, decided to start a new life in Saigon, taking Le Ly with her, while Trong remained in Ky La to care for their land. The mother and daughter first stayed with some former Ky La acquaintances. Le Ly was deeply ashamed that her mother was basically begging these people to take them in. After Le Ly repelled the advances of the teenage boy in the home, the family asked her and Huyen to leave. They found employment and living quarters in the home of a rich Vietnamese family. But when Le Ly—now 16—became pregnant with her employer's child, they had to move again, this time to Da Nang, where Le Ly's sister Lan had an apartment.

Le Ly made money selling Vietnamese crafts and black market goods to American servicemen and soon made enough to move her mother and infant son into their own home.

Two years after leaving Ky La, Le Ly returned there to visit her father. She found Trong too weak to get off his bed, his body covered with bruises. The ARVN, he told her, had falsely accused him of killing American soldiers and had tortured him.

Once she felt confident Trong was in stable condition, Le Ly walked to the top of the hill behind their house where her father had once told her Vietnam's history and her place in it.

The whole area, as far as the eye could see, was destroyed and the village empty of people her age. Many young men had been killed. Young women who couldn't find husbands, not wanting to burden their poverty-stricken parents, had moved to the city for work as housekeepers and hostesses, many of them, including her sister Lan, living with a string of American GI boyfriends. Others had become prostitutes.

Le Ly grieved to think of all the lives the war had destroyed and all the children who would never be born because of it. She wanted to blame someone and told her father so when she reentered the house.

"Are you so smart that you truly know who's to blame?" Trong asked. Everyone on all sides of the war, he said, had been blaming each other from the start. "Don't wonder about right and wrong," he continued. "Right is the goodness you carry in your heart—love for your ancestors and your baby and your family and for everything that lives. Wrong is anything that comes between you and that love. Go back to your little son. Raise him the best way you can. That is the battle you were born to fight. That is the victory you must win."

After he had recuperated, Trong began to visit Le Ly in Da Nang. During one visit, he was in an exceptionally black mood. The VC, he said, had returned to Ky La. They had given him a message for Le Ly: she was to smuggle explosives into Da Nang's American military base.

Trong didn't want her to do it. Le Ly wouldn't even consider it. But Trong wanted her to know what they had requested, he said, in case something happened to him.

He returned to Ky La. He didn't wait for the VC to kill him. He took his own life.

In 1969, when she was 19, Le Ly met a 60-year-old American named Ed Munro, a civilian contractor working with the

Le Ly, age 20.
Le Ly Hayslip

US military in Vietnam. Determined to find a Vietnamese wife, Ed convinced Le Ly to marry him, promising to care for her and her son and to take them away from war-torn Vietnam. They married in 1970, had a baby, and moved to the United States.

When Ed died three years later, Le Ly married a man named Dennis Hayslip, with whom she had a third son.

After returning to Vietnam in 1986 for a visit, Le Ly wrote two memoirs, which Oliver Stone, a filmmaker and Vietnam War veteran, turned into one film called *Heaven and Earth*.

Le Ly eventually founded two humanitarian organizations, the East Meets West Foundation, now called Thrive Networks, and the Global Village Foundation, both designed to help rebuild her war-torn homeland. She is currently retired, living in Southern California, and working on her third book.

LEARN MORE

Child of War, Woman of Peace by Le Ly Hayslip with James Hayslip (Doubleday, 1993).

When Heaven and Earth Changed Places: A Vietnamese Woman's Journey from War to Peace by Le Ly Hayslip with Jay Wurts (Doubleday, 1989).

BOBBI HOVIS

Witness to History

AS US NAVY NURSE BOBBI HOVIS looked out of the plane window, dawn was breaking over South Vietnam. "[The] waterways appeared as silver threads winding in and around rich green rice paddies," she wrote later. It was as lovely, she thought, as "a fine intricate tapestry."

But Bobbi, who had been a medical air evacuation (medevac) nurse during the Korean War, hadn't flown to Vietnam to enjoy its beauty. She was there to work, having received her orders on August 4, 1963.

Immediately after landing in Saigon, Bobbi and the other nurses who had flown with her were escorted into a staff room where they were told in a brief meeting that "anti-American feelings were running high." Bobbi felt a tinge of excitement. It was dangerous, yes, but history was unfolding here. And she would witness it.

The nurses, supporting a larger medical team, were in Saigon to start a combat casualty hospital, which would serve US forces in the area, as well as Vietnamese civilians and military personnel from Australia, New Zealand, the Philippines, and South Korea.

The nurses spent three days in orientation meetings. Major General Charles J. Timmes addressed them first and told them why the Americans were in Vietnam: to stop Ho Chi Minh, the Communist leader of North Vietnam who was trying to unite the country. If Ho succeeded, General Timmes explained, all of Vietnam, North and South, would become Communist, the totalitarian ideology at odds with free Western democracies.

More briefings followed. The nurses were instructed on how to respect Vietnamese customs and avoid attacks from the Vietcong (VC), who could not be easily distinguished from Vietnamese civilians. The nurses were to avoid crowds if at all possible but to stay alert if they suddenly found themselves in the midst of one.

When the orientation ended, the work began. The location for the new hospital was a rickety, filthy apartment building; out of respect to the local Vietnamese, the Americans used existing structures whenever possible.

For several strenuous days, the team sweated in Saigon's oppressive heat as they cleared, swept, swabbed, and sanitized. At last they had an operational 5-floor, 100-bed hospital, complete with emergency and operating rooms.

There was a shingle over the front door of the "new" hospital, dating from its existence as an apartment building, upon which were written the Vietnamese words DUONG DUONG. The medical team had no idea what that meant: their Vietnamese dictionary didn't provide an answer, nor could any of the Vietnamese on their staff. But the name—pronounced, they guessed, "dong dong"—stuck and became the hospital's name.

Shortly after opening, Duong Duong received its first wounded-in-action casualty. Bobbi noticed that the severely

Duong Duong hospital in 1965. *Journal of Navy Medicine*

wounded man wore a green hat. He was a member of the US Army Special Forces, or the Green Berets, named for their distinctive headgear.

The man survived the operation he needed, and Bobbi was proud to be part of this team that had worked together for the first time to save a life. If not for the existence of Duong Duong, Bobbi was certain that the man would have died; he would have been evacuated to the Philippines, and Bobbi didn't think he would have survived the trip.

After being in the intensive care unit for 28 days, the man stabilized and was transferred to a different hospital. When Bobbi said good-bye to him, he placed in her hand his green beret as a gesture of respect and thanks.

"From the day he first arrived at our door, the casualties never ceased—they began to increase proportionately to the escalation of the war effort," Bobbi wrote later. She was convinced that part of the hospital staff's success in saving lives was due to the helicopters, which were able to quickly transport the wounded out of battle zones.

She also credited the excellent work of the Duong Duong team. But this hospital that gave Bobbi so much pride was often difficult to work in. For instance, the elevator constantly broke down, which meant they often had to use the stairways to transport patients between floors. Even when the elevator was supposedly in working order, it could be unreliable: once Bobbi was caught between floors and had to be pulled out by two corpsmen.

"The demand for constant improvisation was indeed frustrating, but it was also rewarding to see just how resourceful we could be," Bobbi wrote later. "Empty intravenous bottles and tubing became drinking containers and straws. . . . Howitzer shell casings of 105 mm made excellent, heavy flower vases."

During her off hours, Bobbi explored Saigon and discovered it to be a city of economic extremes: the wealthy lived in beautiful villas built by the French, while the poor lived on the streets. "At intersections it was common to see an elegant Mercedes sedan confront a lumbering cart pulled by a team of oxen," she wrote.

When Bobbi would sit at an outdoor café, absorbing the city's sights and sounds, she found it difficult to believe there was a war being fought only five miles away. But the very place where she sat was becoming part of that war: the VC began targeting the Saigon cafés that Americans frequented.

One Saturday night the medical staff at Duong Duong admitted several wounded American GIs, victims of a shoe box bomb

Portrait of Bobbi taken by a
local Saigon photographer.
Bobbi Hovis collection

set off in a Saigon bar.
Describing the first vic-
tim, Bobbi wrote, "I have
never witnessed greater
destruction of a human
body, except, perhaps, in
the case of airplane crash
victims." He died within
10 minutes.

But Saigon's chaos
was only beginning. One
October evening, Bobbi was standing on the balcony of her living quarters, looking down onto the street. She saw a taxi pull
to the curb. Out stepped a Buddhist monk, dressed in traditional
robes and carrying a can.

"He proceeded to a spot on the sidewalk and sat down,"
Bobbi wrote later. "Pouring the contents of the can over his
robes, he struck a match and was immediately engulfed in
flames. Even though other monk burnings had occurred, I still
couldn't believe what I was witnessing."

Bobbi called some fellow nurses to join her on the balcony as
she photographed the shocking scene. A large crowd had gathered, but soon police and ARVN soldiers arrived and cordoned
off the area.

Within 30 minutes, the street appeared as if nothing unusual
had occurred there. "The abnormal was becoming normal,"
Bobbi wrote. "The unexpected became the expected."

But on November 1, 1963, something began that was truly extraordinary, even for Saigon. After an uneventful morning, the senior corpsman, returning from lunch some distance away, had shocking news. "There's all kinds of barbed wire strung across the street," he said. "There are gun emplacements set up with .50-caliber machine guns and they're all pointed right up the street at us." Bobbi walked into the street. It was true. Troops were setting up guns and sandbags.

By the time she returned to the hospital, she could hear gunfire. She saw "tree limbs snapping and flying in all directions. Lead was ricocheting off building walls." Planes were dive-bombing the presidential palace. She saw one plane hit by anti-aircraft fire. It went into a dive and disappeared.

The long-rumored coup to overthrow Ngo Dinh Diem, South Vietnam's highly unpopular president, had begun.

Bobbi ran up to the hospital's top-floor balcony so she could watch. She thought the balcony's waist-high balustrade might offer some protection. A corpsman joined her. Fierce gunfire from AK-47s was being exchanged in the street below. All of a sudden, a bullet hit the balustrade right in front of them. It ricocheted to the ceiling and dropped at Bobbi's feet, along with an intense spray of stucco and dust. She and the corpsman ducked and crawled back inside before creeping back out to the balcony to continue watching.

By 5:00 PM Bobbi and several other nurses received permission to return to their living quarters three miles away. The battle had quieted down, although Bobbi described it later as an "uneasy" quiet. She sensed that things "could explode at any moment."

As the evening wore on, the city was blacked out. The local radio station broadcast nothing about the battle. Bobbi wrote later, "The hourly news updates spoke of world events everywhere except where it counted—Saigon. Instead of timely, accurate information on the coup, we listened to the Top 40. It was ominous and ludicrous. I felt that at any moment the blackness would rupture."

At two in the morning, it did. Bobbi heard tanks rolling down the street while shells exploded all around. Their apartment building was "showered with flying tile, glass, and shrapnel. The shells came whistling in, the blast effect tremendous." Still, the women watched from their seventh-floor balcony, taking cover in the stairwell on the fourth floor when the shelling became too intense.

Bobbi then remembered that she owned a shortwave radio. She retrieved it and tuned in to London's BBC, whose broadcaster was discussing the fighting in Saigon but providing no details. "Ironically, we who were sitting in the midst of the fighting were no better informed than the BBC announcer," Bobbi wrote later.

She and the others continued to watch through the moonlit night, observing from the balcony or taking cover in the stairwells. Because their phone line had not been damaged, they assumed there were only minimal casualties arriving at Duong Duong, or else they would have been called to work.

By 3:30 AM the heavy firing died down. Bobbi heard "the clank, clank, clank" of tanks. She crawled out on the balcony and peered down over the railing. "There in the street below, I counted 27 tanks mustering right below our quarters," she wrote. "Several hundred fully armed troops accompanied the tanks." Bobbi was certain this must be their final assault on the presidential palace.

Just before dawn, the sound of gunfire intensified until it was deafening. At that point, the nurse's faces "were blackened with soot." Their eyes burned from "acrid cordite fumes from the explosions of gunpowder," and they all had "pounding headaches" from the noise.

Then, at 6:30 AM, it was over. Bobbi saw a white flag flutter in the distance. She assumed—correctly—that it had been raised over the presidential palace.

When daylight came and the nurses viewed their immediate surroundings, they were surprised their building hadn't taken a direct hit, because the buildings around them certainly had. The roofs, Bobbi wrote, "had holes five feet in diameter. Rubble, roof tiles, and broken glass lay everywhere."

The local radio station finally had some relevant news: President Diem had been overthrown. Cheering crowds filled the streets. Businesses linked to the Diem regime were looted and burned. From their roof on the following day, Bobbi and some other nurses watched showers of pink, green, and yellow leaflets fall from military airplanes into the street below, announcing

A portion of the ruined presidential palace. *Photo by Bobbi Hovis*

the takeover of the new government, the Military Revolutionary Council.

When the nurses arrived at the hospital, the only damage
they noticed were bullet holes in a few walls. Bobbi was amazed
to learn that no patients had been admitted with injuries related
to the coup.

Three weeks later, on November 23, 1963, Bobbi was enjoy-
ing a day off when she tuned her shortwave radio to the Voice
of America broadcast. The station never emitted a completely
clear signal, but she could hear an announcer repeatedly mention the word "assassination." Who had been the target? After
hearing the name Kennedy more than once, Bobbi was horrified to realize that John F. Kennedy, the president of the United
States, had been shot.

The following day, she and her friends were profoundly
moved to see thousands of Vietnamese students carrying pro-
Kennedy placards in a solemn procession. A sudden deluge of
rain didn't stop them.

Bobbi hoped the regime change in South Vietnam might
shorten the war. But in her opinion, "the war effort was deteriorating from bad to worse." On January 30, 1964, Ambassador
Lodge spoke over the Armed Forces Radio Service. He warned
American personnel to stay on duty or in their quarters; the
streets of Saigon were too dangerous.

Days later, leaflets appeared all over Saigon with this message: "Two Americans a Day." Frightening rumors circulated:
poison darts aimed at American necks, bounties for the capture
of navy nurses. Bobbi and the others began to wear civilian
clothing to and from the hospital.

On the night of February 16, 1964, Bobbi and two friends
intended to see a film at the Capital Kinh Do Theater, but a last-
minute dinner invitation caused them to change their plans.

The VC targeted the theater that night. Hearing the explosion, the nurses raced to the hospital. Duong Duong was in chaos, crammed with wounded civilians, their frantic family members, reporters, investigators, and military police.

Gurneys were rushed into the emergency and operating rooms six or seven at a time. "I had never seen so many casualties at once," Bobbi wrote later.

After working for 36 hours straight, she left the hospital and stopped at the theater, now a mess of "twisted metal, shattered glass, huge slabs of ceiling plaster."

Then she saw something that left her "limp" and sent "a cold chill" down her spine. The seat where she usually sat—ten rows from the back on the aisle so she could be easily located in case of a hospital emergency—was completely blown away.

On the night of April 4 an American helicopter pilot still wearing his flight suit was admitted to Duong Duong on a stretcher. Bobbi took his pulse. He didn't have one. In the dead man's pocket she found a photo of a pretty young woman and two little girls. Bobbi's eyes filled with tears. During the past seven months of nursing casualties, she had never reacted in this way. She knew she had reached a "saturation point." These Americans, she wrote later, "were among the best of our young soldiers, volunteers who had chosen to serve in Vietnam." It seemed tragic that they were now dying on foreign soil.

Bobbi put that emotional moment behind her and worked to the end of her yearlong tour of duty. Days before her October 10 departure, she and the other homeward-bound medics were given a surprise going-away party. But the biggest surprise came when General William Westmoreland, commander of the Military Assistance Command, Vietnam (MACV), and General John L. Throckmorton, deputy commander of MACV, walked into the party to personally thank the medics for their service.

On November 1, 1967, Bobbi retired from the Navy Corps. During her 20-plus years of service, she received multiple awards, including many for her year in Vietnam. Her most recent award, a Distinguished Citizen Medal from the Daughters of the American Revolution, came in October 2014.

But while she appreciates the honors, Bobbi maintains that the work itself was always her best reward: "The care of these patients in the war was my main purpose in life and doing it was great satisfaction for me."

In 1992 she used the letters she wrote to her mother during her year in Saigon as the basis of a memoir.

Bobbi was the first woman to fly a navy jet and logged nearly 1,500 hours in military hospital planes and helicopters, as well as 250 hours in private planes. She remains active to this day, flying a biplane once per year as a birthday present to herself.

LEARN MORE

Americans at War by the Naval Institute Press, www.youtube.com/watch?v=YVYsET0OZPk.
An interview with Bobbi about her service and time in Vietnam.

"Around Annapolis: 1st Navy Nurse Corps Officer to Volunteer for Vietnam Honored by DAR" by Aries Matheos, *Capital Gazette*, October 31, 2014, www.capitalgazette.com/neighborhoods/ph-ac-cc-around-annapolis-1031-20141031-story.html.

Station Hospital Saigon: A Navy Nurse in Vietnam, 1963–1964 by Bobbi Hovis (Naval Institute Press, 1992).

Part III
1965–1968

LYNDON B. JOHNSON'S AMERICAN WAR

★

ON MARCH 8, 1965, 3,500 US Marines landed near the shore of the central Vietnamese city of Da Nang, the first American combat troops to arrive in Vietnam. There to secure the Da Nang air base, the marines were a visible symbol of America's increasing resolve to support the government in South Vietnam against the Communists.

Meanwhile, the Northern government in Hanoi was making determinations of its own, mobilizing its economy and people for the war effort. Although Hanoi officials would deny it for years, tens of thousands of North Vietnamese Army (NVA) soldiers had already been moving south by way of a network of jungle pathways collectively known as Ho Chi Minh Trail. Along with the NVA soldiers came weapons, supplies, and ammunition, which would also support the soldiers of the People's

Liberation Armed Forces (PLAF)—known by their enemies as the Vietcong (VC)—in the South.

Although the Vietnamese population knew exactly where the fighting was, the same could not be said for most Americans at the time: few could even locate Vietnam on a map. Nevertheless, Americans did understand that Communist-controlled nations, such as those in Eastern Europe and China, did not have the freedoms enjoyed in democracies. Despite US senator Joseph McCarthy's chilling anti-Communist crusade throughout the 1950s—which destroyed the careers and reputations of thousands of Americans and caused a cloud of fear and suspicion to fall over the country—US citizens realized that nations implementing Communism were oppressive, totalitarian regimes intolerant of dissent, frighteningly similar to the Fascist states the United States and its allies had defeated during World War II. And most Americans were willing to support a war that fought the ideology they considered to be the world's new threat: a poll taken in 1965 revealed that a majority of them approved of sending combat troops to Vietnam.

The marine landing at Da Nang, though a dramatic moment, wouldn't be nearly enough to keep Saigon from falling to the Communists. US general William Westmoreland, commander of the Military Assistance Command, Vietnam (MACV), told President Lyndon B. Johnson that he would need 180,000 men total for defensive measures in South Vietnam. To do more—that is, to mount successful offensives called search-and-destroy missions against the VC hidden in the countryside—he would need an additional 100,000 soldiers.

If the United States was, as it claimed, only present to support the South in its fight to remain free of the North, why did the military need such large numbers of American fighting men? Because the Southern military commanding the Army of

COMMUNISM

Communism is an ideology in which a society's economy—that is, its wealth and means of producing goods—is directly controlled by its citizens. The idea grew out of the French Revolution, when, in the late 18th century, poverty-stricken peasants successfully rose up against wealthy aristocrats. But German political philosopher Karl Marx was the first to detail the idea in writing, during the mid to late 19th century; in western nations, the industrial revolution had made business owners wealthy at the expense of their overworked and underpaid employees, many of whom were school-age children.

Marx and his associate Friedrich Engels envisioned a classless society in which everyone would labor to the best of their abilities and be provided for, whether or not they were able to work. Communism, as originally intended, has been practiced by some utopian, religious, and tribal societies throughout history. But the nations that have claimed to establish Communist governments—beginning with the former Soviet Union—have ultimately been responsible for a tragic number of human rights abuses. Why? These nations' economies have never been managed by the people of those nations. Rather, power has always fallen into the hands of leaders who establish autocratic regimes supported and enforced by a privileged ruling class of loyal Communist Party members. These leaders and party members not only control the economy but also severely limit freedom of speech, religion, and political opinion. Citizens of Communist nations who attempt to exercise any one of these freedoms contrary to the dictates of their government—or who are even suspected of doing so—are imprisoned, forced into labor camps, or executed. To date, the number of people murdered by their own Communist-controlled governments exceeds 100 million.

the Republic of Vietnam (ARVN) was ineffective and unable to convey the same nationalistic zeal that was inspiring its enemies. Southern military officers seemed to be interested more in bickering with each other than in fighting the VC. Most were granted positions based on a corrupt reward system, not on skill or experience. ARVN soldiers, required to serve for the duration of the war, were given little motivation to remain loyal to their corrupt leaders, and they deserted by the thousands—often temporarily, to care for their families or receive treatment for battle wounds.

As more Americans came to Vietnam, they radically altered the character of the South's capital city. Saigon retained its French architecture, but its identity was becoming increasingly American. Shops and businesses were created to cater to the foreigners, and Saigon's economy became as dependent on the Americans as the Southern military was.

Despite the shaky foundation upon which the United States was building this war, a general spirit of optimism ran through the US news broadcasts about the conflict: the search-and-destroy missions against the VC were as effective, reporters said, as Operation Rolling Thunder, the bombing campaign against the North that had begun on March 2, 1965. It was only a matter of time, proclaimed the reports, before the United States would receive offers of surrender from North Vietnam.

That opinion received a blow three years later on January 21, 1968, however, when 20,000 NVA soldiers began their siege of the US air base outside the central Vietnamese city of Khe Sanh. Americans' optimism was absolutely devastated nine days later; in the early morning hours of January 30, 70,000 Communist fighters—NVA and VC—attacked more than 100 Southern cities, towns, and military bases in what became known as the Tet Offensive because it began on Tet, the Vietnamese New Year.

The offensive—a complete surprise because the Communists had agreed to a cease-fire during this important national holiday—was a defeat for both sides. The Communists had hoped their show of military strength would rally Southern ers to their side as they rose up together against the Americans and the Southern government. This didn't happen. And what occurred in the Southern city of Hue during the Tet Offensive made the South Vietnamese fear, rather than welcome, the idea of a Northern takeover: while Hue was in their control, Communist forces conducted a brutal massacre of at least 3,000 previously targeted Vietnamese civilians.

The Communist forces were defeated in a matter of weeks. And because the VC had suffered greater losses than the NVA, the government in Hanoi realized it would have to send even more NVA troops south down Ho Chi Minh Trail.

Yet, in one important way, the Tet Offensive was a victory for the Communists: it signaled the end of American optimism regarding the Vietnam War by making it obvious that the Communist effort in the South was still strong. This war clearly had no end in sight.

And 1968 would bring more bad news to Americans. On April 4, 1968, Martin Luther King Jr., beloved civil rights leader and promoter of nonviolent civil disobedience, was assassinated. He had not only led his fellow African Americans in the struggle to end legalized racism but also publicly criticized US involvement in Vietnam as immoral.

News of his assassination was met with riots in more than 100 American cities; 43 people were killed, 3,500 injured, and entire city blocks destroyed. Army troops were called to the nation's capital to restore order. In some instances, racial tensions erupted into fights within the integrated American forces stationed in Vietnam.

President Johnson, devastated by the Tet Offensive, had announced in March that he would not seek a second term in that year's election. By that time two challengers for the Democratic presidential nomination had already stepped forward—Senators Eugene McCarthy and Robert F. Kennedy, brother of the slain president. The strong antiwar stance of these two senators had put President Johnson in the extremely uncomfortable position of appearing prowar.

When Senator Kennedy was gunned down by an assassin on June 5, minutes after winning the California primary, hopes of the United States pulling out of Vietnam were that much dimmer, and the nation seemed to be drowning in violence. One young police officer named Dennis Pierson claimed Kennedy's death made many Americans believe that "there was no more law, order, or even sanity" in their country.

That summer's continued violence proved this bleak outlook to be painfully accurate.

Antiwar activists decided to bring their message to the streets of Chicago; the city would be the focus of the nation's attention during the Democratic National Convention. Knowing that the protestors were on their way and threatening violent disruptions, the Chicago police force was there to meet them in unusually large numbers, along with members of the Illinois National Guard.

The protestors despised the police and guardsmen, viewing them as ignorant supporters of a nation conducting an immoral war. The police, many of whom were veterans of previous wars, despised the protestors in equal measure, considering them to be spoiled, privileged, and—as they often burned flags as a symbol of protest—profoundly anti-American.

Violent clashes erupted, with neither side appearing in a positive light. The activists knew they would have to lie low until they could reemerge with more effective plans that might benefit the movement.

Hubert Humphrey, the politician nominated as the presidential candidate at the Democratic National Convention, narrowly lost the presidential election to Republican Richard M. Nixon, a politician who during his campaign had pledged "an honorable end to the war in Vietnam."

KAY WILHELMY BAUER

American Survivor

LATE IN 1965, 28 YEAR-OLD Kay Wilhelmy was at the large Great Lakes Naval Hospital in Illinois explaining to its director of nursing service (DNS) that she was leaving the navy. After seven years of military service, she wanted to do mission work and had just accepted a position as director of a school of nursing in South America. The DNS at Great Lakes had other ideas for her. "Kay, just a minute," she interrupted. "You have been in the Far East, haven't you?"

Kay had. Before coming to Great Lakes in 1963, she had worked in naval hospitals in Guam and Japan, where she'd spent many off-duty hours with missionaries providing health care to local citizens.

The DNS explained that the navy was assembling a Vietnam-bound surgical team. Kay was aware of what was going on in that country: for the past two years she and the other Great Lakes nurses had pored daily over reports of those missing and killed in action, hoping the names of the young hospital corpsmen they knew would not appear. Too often they did. Many of these young men had been like younger brothers to the nurses, who had thrown bridal and baby showers for their wives. Kay and the other nurses at Great Lakes had also spent many tragic hours consoling these young women when they became widows.

Now Kay was being ordered into this war zone. She listened as the DNS called Washington, DC. She was assigned to a seven-member surgical team going to Kien Giang Province, in far South Vietnam, where there was currently no US military hospital. When not working with US casualties, the team would provide surgical care for the Vietnamese military and civilians at the Vietnamese Provincial Hospital in the city of Rach Gia, capital of the Kien Giang Province.

The surgical team would include a navy orthopedic surgeon, a navy general surgeon, a senior navy operating room nurse/instructor, a navy chief who was a laboratory and X-ray technician, a US Air Force nurse anesthetist, a US Army medical service officer, and Kay.

When Kay called home from Great Lakes to tell her parents about her new plans, her mother asked if she really wanted to go to Vietnam.

"I think so," Kay answered. While that answer satisfied her mother, her father was clearly not pleased with his eldest daughter's plans. Kay could hear him in the background shouting, "There's a &%$+ war going on there!"

When the team first touched down in Saigon, in January 1966, several things made clear just how accurate his words had been. First, they learned that only a few weeks earlier, eight US Navy nurses had received Purple Heart medals for being wounded during a mortar attack on the Saigon Naval Hospital there. And the team, Kay was surprised to learn, would wear camouflage while working, not their usual white uniforms.

Kay giving shots on a nearby island after an outbreak of the plague.
Kay Wilhelmy Bauer

The French had built the province hospital in Rach Gia during the early 20th century. There was no running water; the only water supply was rainwater that collected in cement cisterns outside. While the operating room ran on generator-provided electricity, the rest of the hospital had none. And the windows had no screens.

But the medics made it work, and when a wounded US serviceman was brought in, they conducted the three Ts, as they called it: triage, treat, and transport. That is, they would first make a decision regarding the odds of the man's survival. If he could be saved, they quickly decided which type of emergency treatment to give before sending him by plane to the nearest US-run hospital.

The nurses soon made the acquaintance of Sergeant Phu, a medic from the Army of the Republic of Vietnam (ARVN) who was fluent in several languages and who translated for them whenever necessary. One day Sergeant Phu presented them

with a problem: the wives and children of the ARVN, being neither technically civilians nor members of the military, couldn't
receive treatment from the civilian doctor in the area nor the
ARVN doctor.

Sergeant Phu proposed an idea to the nurses: if he and his
medics built a new clinic for these women and children, would
they agree to visit it once per week? The answer was yes, and
once a week Kay and Brenda, the senior operating room nurse,
examined and cared for everyone who visited the clinic. If anyone required further treatment, the nurses referred that patient
to the Vietnamese chief of medicine or the navy surgeons.

On several occasions Sergeant Phu asked Kay and Brenda to
visit a different clinic, this one in the jungle in a Vietcong (VC)–
controlled area. Many sick and wounded Vietnamese were
unable or afraid to travel through this territory to the province
hospital for treatment. Were Kay and Brenda willing to do what
the sick Vietnamese were not?

Sergeant Phu told them that a scout party would go ahead of
them and Kay and Brenda would be escorted by his men. Plus,
he said, everyone knew the American medical team was there
to care for all Vietnamese people, regardless of their loyalties or
affiliation, so there was little risk of the Americans being targeted.

Kay agreed but was still a bit apprehensive—until the uni-
formed escort arrived. These ARVN men were heavily armed
with rockets and plenty of ammunition for their M14 rifles.
Their destination was a green building marked with a large red
cross on a white roof to identify it as a medical facility. There
Kay and Brenda treated civilians for ringworm and internal
parasites—common ailments in the area—along with wounds
received from mines and other explosives.

Back in the relative safety of Rach Gia, Kay and the team
were involved with far more serious cases. The VC had laid

mines along the roads connecting cities in the area. Whenever a bus hit one of these mines, the surviving passengers—civilians or soldiers—would be taken to the province hospital. They were frequently covered in mud—the explosions often sent them flying into the nearby rice paddies—so the medical team had to first sponge them off, using buckets of water brought in from the outdoor cisterns, before they could assess the wounds.

Danger from the VC was always near but never predictable. One day Kay and a nurse named Kathie accepted an invitation to watch a film at an ARVN compound in nearby Rach Soi. A US Army captain who was training an ARVN unit there had a generator, a projector, and a new American film he wanted to show the two nurses.

The film was so engrossing none of them noticed that darkness was falling outside. Travel after nightfall was risky. While Rach Soi was only a 15-minute drive from Rach Gia, it was a very dangerous 15 minutes: they might be attacked by VC as they bounced their way along the rutted road in their jeep, but they were in equal danger from ARVN soldiers who guarded the road into Rach Gia after sundown and might mistake them for VC in the dark.

Kay and Kathie, to their great relief, returned safely to their quarters. Their phone was ringing when they arrived. It was the hospital. The Rach Soi compound had been partially blown up: while they had been watching the movie inside, the VC had laid claymore mines outside. The casualties—ARVN personnel and their families—were being transported to the hospital, and the nurses were needed immediately. The medical team worked all that night and saved many lives.

Just before the team's yearlong tour of duty was over, the Republic of Vietnam decorated each of them with the Humanitarian Service Medal.

Kay after receiving the
Humanitarian Service Medal
in 1966. *Kay Wilhelmy Bauer*

As they prepared to
leave, they were given
some chilling advice: travel
in civilian clothes, and
don't tell any fellow trav-
elers where you've been.
American war protestors
were targeting returning
veterans with verbal and
physical abuse.

So Kay made sure
every aspect of her appearance looked unmistakably
civilian before boarding
her first plane. But on her second flight, a male flight attendant
asked her if she had just returned from Vietnam. "I was so surprised, I . . . quickly scanned myself to see if I looked military,
but could find nothing amiss," Kay said later. "I was afraid to say
yes, but worried about saying no."

She told him the truth and discovered he had no intention of
harassing her. Quite the opposite: he wanted to honor her with
steak and ice cream and a special seat assignment!

After two weeks' leave at home in St. Paul, Minnesota, in
February 1967, Kay was sent to the naval hospital at the marine
base in Quantico, Virginia. She had many duties there but

especially enjoyed working with marines who had just returned from Vietnam; her interactions with them helped both Kay and the marines process their recent experiences.

Later that year Quantico's chief nurse called Kay to her office. Kay was going to the White House, the chief told her. President Lyndon B. Johnson had invited 20 military women to be present when he signed the H.R. 5894 bill, which removed restrictions on how far women could advance within the ranks of the military.

Kay represented the US Navy Nurse Corps at the ceremony, and President Johnson signed the bill with multiple pens so each woman present could take one home.

Three months later, in February 1968, Kay was assigned to recruiting duty in Minneapolis, Minnesota, the "sister city" of her hometown, St. Paul. Kay often accompanied male navy recruiters when they visited college campuses; the presence of a female sometimes diminished harassment from war protestors. When protestors confronted Kay, she would say, "Wait a minute. I just got back from Vietnam. Let me tell you what is going on there. If you don't like the war, don't talk to us. Talk to those who sign bills about war, your congressmen and your representatives."

She may not have been responsible for the war, but Kay's uniform and her job as a recruiter made her one of its tangible symbols to those who were actively opposing it. And for that, she nearly paid the ultimate price.

On the morning of August 17, 1970, Kay received a shocking telephone call from her commanding officer telling her to stay home. A bomb had been detonated on the steps directly outside Kay's office door. She had survived a year in a war zone, but here, in what she thought was the safety of her home state, Kay's life was in danger!

Kay with President Lyndon B. Johnson on November 8, 1967.
Kay Wilhelmy Bauer

A few months later, on the evening of October 4, she was watching television in her St. Paul home with Amy, her former roommate and longtime friend. Vern Bauer, Kay's husband of four months, had already gone to bed. Suddenly Kay and Amy heard the sound of an explosion, and the house began to shake.

Kay went outside. The house next door had blown up. Fragments had landed on Kay's roof and in her front and back yards. The blast had also dislodged a heavy oak door in Kay's house and slammed it into the hallway, narrowly missing Vern, who had been awoken by the explosion.

The next-door neighbors, asleep in their bed, had been killed instantly.

As Kay stood outside with the stunned crowd watching the burning remnants of the house, a man in a suit and tie tapped her on the shoulder.

"Are you LCDR [Lieutenant Commander] Bauer?" he asked.

"Who wants to know?" Kay said.

He showed Kay his badge, as did another man, also in a suit and tie, standing next to him. They were from the Office of Naval Intelligence. They told Kay that because the two incidents had occurred within two months, she needed to move away. In the meantime, she was to stop driving a navy car to and from work.

The next day the newspaper headlines related the blast incident. Inside one paper was a short, chilling article titled "'Wrong House' Idea Considered in Blast." Although many of the neighbors believed the explosion had been an accident involving a faulty gas hookup, the Office of Naval Intelligence told Kay, Vern, and Amy that the remains of an explosive device had been discovered behind the refrigerator in the neighbors' house.

While the terrorists who blew up Kay's office were eventually caught, those who destroyed her neighbors' home and took their lives were never found.

Kay reluctantly resigned her active military duty when she left her recruiting work in 1971 and accepted a Reserve commission; she and Vern wanted to adopt a child, but adoption agencies refused to allow active-duty female military personnel to become adoptive parents. In 1972 she and Vern adopted a one-year-old boy named Jeffery, and 11 months later, Kay gave birth to a son, whom they named Terry.

About 10 years after her Vietnam tour of duty, Kay began to have war-related flashbacks. For instance, during a Good Friday service, when her church was darkened and the simulated sounds of thunder and lightning filled the sanctuary, Kay suddenly saw in her mind's eye helicopters filled with wounded men approaching the hospital in Rach Gia. She had to remind herself where she actually was. Similar incidents began to force their way into her consciousness with alarming suddenness.

To cope, Kay began to distance herself from her emotions. While she could chat with anyone about almost any topic, she kept her feelings private. Her emotional detachment started to affect her marriage, and Vern eventually gave her an ultimatum: they should seek counseling together, or he would divorce her. They went together for marriage counseling and stayed together, but Kay still didn't feel the need to seek any therapy for herself, even as she continually urged her Vietnam veteran friends to get tested for post-traumatic stress disorder (PTSD). Finally, one fellow Vietnam veteran agreed to get tested only if Kay did, and she relented.

Kay tested positive for PTSD and sought professional help. While recovering, she became part of a Minnesota-based team, headed by fellow Vietnam nurse veteran Diane Carlson Evans, that sought to build a national monument in Washington, DC, dedicated to the American women who served in the Vietnam

POST-TRAUMATIC STRESS DISORDER

Post-traumatic stress disorder (PTSD) occurs when a person exposed to a traumatic event, such as combat, continues to suffer severe stress connected to that event long after it has passed. People with PTSD can experience recurring nightmares about the past trauma, or they can unexpectedly find themselves reliving it during waking hours when an unrelated situation triggers the memory. PTSD sufferers will often try to avoid situations that set off such reactions, but they may react with rage or despair when they occur. PTSD has affected combat military personnel throughout history but was first given its name in the 1970s in connection to the postwar sufferings of Vietnam veterans.

War. Kay was the committee secretary for their weekly meetings, and when the effort grew and Diane traveled the country to gain wider national support, Kay and other Minneapolis nurse veterans did what they could to support the effort locally.

It took 10 difficult years, overcoming countless roadblocks, passing two pieces of Congressional legislation, and winning the approval of three federal commissions, but the Vietnam Women's Memorial was finally unveiled on November 11, 1993.

The dedication ceremony included a parade of Vietnam veteran nurses who Kay remembers were "overwhelmed by the number of people who lined the streets waving flags and shouting cheers." Some male Vietnam veterans rushed out to thank the nurses, and Kay even witnessed some actual reunions right in the middle of the parade.

In addition to working on the monument effort, Kay helped establish the Minnesota Association of Civilian and Veteran Women. While involved in these two projects, she crossed paths with many Vietnam War nurse veterans who were suffering from varying levels of PTSD, and she decided to do something to help them, starting a local group that met on the grounds of the Minnesota Veterans Administration Medical Center (VAMC). "The VAMC at that time put all Vietnam vets in an outbuilding as we were 'too crazy' to be in the hospital," recalls Kay. But she persisted until the VAMC finally allowed her to initiate a PTSD program specifically for these women veterans. The Minneapolis VAMC is now one of the top centers of its kind, she says, and its exemplary women's program is emulated by many other VAMCs in the country.

She was also instrumental in founding the Minnesota Women Veterans Association, which now has several hundred members. And although currently fighting cancer, Kay continues to stay involved with Vietnam nurse veterans to this day.

THE VIETNAM WOMEN'S MEMORIAL

Excerpt from the speech given on November 11, 1993, by Diane Carlson Evans, captain, Army Nurse Corps 1966–1972, Vietnam 1968–1969, and founder and president of the Vietnam Women's Memorial Foundation: "We have just unveiled the first monument in the history of the United States of America dedicated in our nation's capital to American women who served during wartime. Welcome home daughters of America. Welcome home my fellow sister veterans. Allow the love and pride that fill this hallowed space to enter your hearts and souls today and forever as we continue on our journey in life."

The Vietnam Women's Memorial in Washington, DC. *Noreen Lake*

 LEARN MORE

"Catherine (Kay) M. Bauer" by Kay Bauer, in *Vietnam War Nurses: Personal Accounts of 18 Americans*, edited by Patricia Rushton (McFarland, 2013).

Sisterhood of War: Minnesota Women in Vietnam by Kim Heikkila (Minnesota Historical Society Press, 2011).

JURATE KAZICKAS

"What's a Woman Like You Doing Out Here?"

WHEN JURATE KAZICKAS told her parents she was headed to Vietnam to report on the war, her mother began weeping. "Everything we have done in life was to keep you from ever having to live through a war again," she said through her tears.

While growing up in New York City, Jurate had learned by heart her family's World War II tale. Her father, Joseph Kazickas, had been an active and well-known member of the anti-Communist resistance in Vilnius, Lithuania's capital. So when the Soviets entered the city in June 1944, Joseph fled in the middle of the night with his wife, Alexandra, and Jurate, their 18-month-old daughter.

Their difficult and terrifying journey—most of it on foot— was filled with many close calls. For instance, during a long train ride, they surely would have been caught by Soviet authorities constantly on the alert for fleeing refugees if not for the kindness of German soldiers who hid the family under piles of bandages.

The train's last stop was the German city of Dresden, which the Kazickas family then left on February 13, 1945, just hours before the Allies began to destroy it. Jurate's parents never forgot the sight of Dresden's destruction, as from a distance they observed "raging fires that filled the sky."

The family eventually wound up in an American-run displaced persons camp in Germany where GIs showered curly-headed little Jurate with candy, calling her Shirley Temple. Finally, in 1947 Joseph, Alexandra, and Jurate sailed across the Atlantic Ocean to New York City on the USS *Ernie Pyle*, named for a famous World War II reporter who had lost his life while covering the war in the Pacific.

Now, with the grown-up Jurate determined to go to Vietnam, Alexandra was afraid her daughter might share Pyle's fate and could not understand what compelled Jurate to actively seek out war. Jurate would never be quite sure herself what had drawn her there, but she thought perhaps her family's story, instead of giving her an aversion to war, had made her feel it was an essential part of who she was.

Vietnam had first piqued Jurate's interest in 1965. While traveling alone through Asia on a hiking vacation, she met some American GIs on leave in Bangkok, Thailand. They all spoke about the "crazy, terrifying world" they had just left, their war against a frustratingly "unseen enemy" who hid in "lush jungles, rice paddies, and villages."

Jurate immediately headed for Saigon, a city she found fascinating, an odd mixture of American and Vietnamese culture where the sounds of war could be heard in the distance. Writing later, she said, "Something was planted in my soul during that day and night as I careened through the bustling streets. . . . I knew that I would return one day. A new and mysterious world was beckoning."

Jurate at the fire support base with the soldiers of the 1st Battalion, 12th Infantry Regiment. *Jurate Kazickas*

Back in New York, Jurate energetically researched the war. But when she felt ready to go, she couldn't find a news outlet or magazine willing to send her: they wanted a war correspondent, and Jurate had no publishing credentials. So she decided to go as a freelancer, paying her own travel expenses. When three news organizations agreed to at least consider her work if she produced anything, Jurate was granted official accreditation with the US military.

In June 1967 she hopped off a marine helicopter with her camera and heavy rucksack onto a landing zone in north-central Vietnam. She was to accompany a group of marines who had just left their combat base in Khe Sanh. On a secret patrol, they were headed toward the Laotian border, six miles away, where they planned to disrupt a suspected enemy supply route of the North Vietnamese Army (NVA).

Jurate didn't dare let the young marines know how exhausted she found the first day's march up and down hills, through bamboo, 10-foot-high razor-edged "elephant" grass, and a river full of leeches. She even pretended not to notice when one of the men strapped extra ammunition weighing seven and a half pounds around her already heavy pack. "Hardcore!" they laughed admiringly as Jurate marched up the next hill without comment or complaint.

The marines might have played tricks like this on her, but Jurate found the young men endearing. "Watching them kidding around with one another, sharing letters from home, proudly showing off pictures of their sweethearts, I was always struck by how young and vulnerable they were," she wrote later. "The thought that some of them might never come home from Vietnam was too terrible to contemplate. But I knew it was true. And so did they."

During a rest stop, one of them—who called Jurate Sam, claiming her real name was too difficult to remember—asked, "What's a woman like you doing out here?"

She replied, "I'm a reporter, and this is the biggest story of our times. I want to experience what's going on here so my reports will be accurate and truthful."

When another young marine, listening to their conversation, heard that Jurate was a freelance reporter and hadn't been specifically assigned to Vietnam, he cried, "You mean you came over here on your own just to get shot at? Wow! Sam, you're nuts!"

Then, more seriously, he continued, "What do you think about all this? You one of those peaceniks that tell everybody we should get the hell out of this place?"

Jurate was still forming her opinion on the war, but at that moment she said no, she was not a "peacenik." "My country was taken away from me by the Communists," she explained. "I know what it is like to be denied freedom."

Jurate, the men, and their company commander, Captain Franklin Delano Bynum, had to part company too soon. Captain Bynum had insisted Jurate have a personal escort before he agreed to take her along. His unfortunate choice had been an out-of-shape staff sergeant desk clerk who couldn't keep up with them and eventually pulled a muscle. Captain Bynum ordered an evacuation helicopter for the sergeant and insisted that Jurate leave with him. She protested: she had kept up with the marches and had been promised a five-day patrol. But her objections meant nothing in the face of marine regulations.

She knew she had gained Captain Bynum's respect, however: as her helicopter flew away and the marines nearby turned their heads away from its dusty downdraft, the captain faced it, stood at attention, and saluted Jurate good-bye.

A few days later, she received word that he had been killed, and she couldn't bring herself to write the story of his company and their patrol. She felt responsible for his death: surely her evacuation helicopter had alerted the area's NVA soldiers to the company's location.

Back in the relative safety of Saigon, Jurate pondered her next move. She felt lonely. Although there were male journalists in the city, she usually avoided them, never feeling quite comfortable with what she called that "journalistic fraternity." Most of her male colleagues seemed to share the attitude of military men toward female reporters, and Jurate was asked more than once, "What the hell is a woman doing in a war zone?"

But she did not let the implications of that question stand in her way. A few months later, in August 1967, she accompanied the army's 101st Airborne Division. Their mission was to search an area filled with enemy fortifications that had been heavily bombed the night before.

Although Jurate didn't think anyone could have possibly survived the air bombardment, clearly someone had: shortly after the Americans entered the area, they came under NVA sniper fire.

The Americans—and Jurate—dove into some nearby trenches. She could hear the sound of bullets flying overhead.

At one point during the two-hour-long firefight, she emerged from the trenches to witness a scene that moved her deeply. An American soldier named Rob had been shot in the back and was lying on the ground. He couldn't get up. He called out to his friend Daniel. Daniel ran through the rice paddy toward Rob, zigzagging to avoid enemy fire. He found Rob and pulled him to safety.

Jurate had interviewed Daniel earlier, and he had told her he had come to Vietnam hoping he might save a life. She wrote later, thinking of Daniel, "War, for all its brutality and horror, nevertheless offered men an opportunity like no other to be fearless and brave, to be selfless, to be a hero."

She was also impressed with the deep platonic love she often witnessed between fighting men. One day she was observing a close-range firefight between the NVA and the 173rd Airborne Brigade on a hill when an NVA rocket exploded in the midst of the Americans. Hot shrapnel flew in all directions. Wounded Americans screamed in agony.

Specialist Jerl Withers, tears in his eyes, tried to help the wounded and begged them to stop screaming, saying they were encouraging the enemy.

"Don't worry, man," he said, holding one severely wounded soldier while attempting to bandage his head. "You're going to be all right. You're going to be home soon, right? Can you hear me? Say something, man. Say something. Please God, please help."

"The moment was so intimate, so raw, so tender, it took my breath away," Jurate wrote later.

There were so many serious casualties the medics couldn't get to them all. Jurate put her camera away and asked if she could help. A busy medic pushed some bandages toward her and gestured to a group of wounded men.

Later that night, back in her clean Saigon room, Jurate's mind was filled with the "terrifying visions" of the day. Her emotions were in turmoil: "Without the companionship of the men when I was out in the field, the sadness and loneliness I felt during those midnight hours in Saigon was wrenching, as if I had lost every friend I ever had. I had no one I could turn to and talk to about my fear and confusion. I could not make sense of this war, nor did I know why I still wanted to stay."

Her doubts about her country's role in the war were growing. "American soldiers were battling for possession of the same hill again and again, sacrificing so many lives for worthless terrain," she wrote later. "Despite my loathing of communism and my belief that we could not walk away from the South Vietnamese who had asked for our help, I too began to feel the war was a terrible mistake, a sacrifice too great for any country, including my own, to bear."

Late in 1967 Jurate's attention again turned toward the marine base at Khe Sanh. US intelligence reported that 40,000 NVA soldiers were headed in that direction. The US military fortified the base with weapons, ammunition, and 6,000 additional marines.

On January 21, 1968, NVA forces besieged the base, which puzzled the US military command. The mystery was cleared up on January 31, 1968, the Vietnamese Tet holiday, when the Communists attacked over 100 Southern cities and towns. The attack on Khe Sanh Combat Base had obviously been designed to divert manpower and ammunition from Saigon and the other Southern cities.

After Tet the NVA continued its siege of Khe Sanh. President Lyndon B. Johnson became unnerved, fearing this battle might lose the war for the United States, as the siege at Dien Bien Phu had cost France the previous war.

The battle of Khe Sanh became one of the longest and bloodiest single battles of the Vietnam War. Every combat journalist wanted to be there. But because it was surrounded by the NVA, trips in and out were dangerous and the press limited to a quota system: only 10 reporters were allowed on the base at one time. Most of these spots were filled with reporters officially associated with the wire services and television networks.

But this was one situation in which being a female reporter had distinct advantages. Jurate already knew that just by hanging around an airstrip, she could often catch a ride from some obliging young helicopter pilot who liked the idea of having a female traveler on board—even if she didn't have the proper authorization. "What are they going to do?" said one pilot when Jurate asked if he might get in trouble on her behalf. "Send me to Vietnam?"

On March 7 Jurate arrived at the Khe Sanh base, ahead of a long waiting list of journalists. It had been quiet for several days, and she was recording marine interviews for a New York radio station. The marines were relaxed, and the battle seemed to be winding down.

She had just clicked on her tape recorder when, as she described it later, "the unmistakable high-pitched whistling sound of an incoming artillery round shattered the air. Frantic voices all over the base shouted, 'Incoming!'" The shell landed only 20 yards from where Jurate was standing.

Someone grabbed her arm and ran her toward a bunker. Another shell hit, this one even closer. The explosion knocked Jurate to the ground, and she crawled the rest of the way into the bunker. It was pitch-black inside. Her legs felt numb. She touched her pants. They were sticky with blood. She felt her face. It was dry and covered with little bumps.

After Jurate was evacuated to a nearby medical bunker, doctors removed a piece of shrapnel embedded in her back, dangerously close to her spine. She was relocated with others who had been wounded that day, and another doctor painstakingly removed each tiny piece of shrapnel embedded in her face.

During her weeklong recuperation, Jurate wondered anew why war had such a powerful "subliminal pull" on her. "I seemed inexorably drawn to be on the front lines, to see and feel the drama of the battlefield. . . . Sometimes I wondered if perhaps I even wanted to be a soldier," she wrote.

But following her release from the hospital, Jurate knew her relationship to war had undergone a drastic transformation. She discovered that she could no longer function calmly under fire, later saying, "Getting wounded had jolted me to the inescapable truth that I was just as vulnerable as any of the thousands of other GIs who were casualties of this war."

When she returned to the United States, she felt torn by the antiwar movement. Although she too was "passionate about seeing an end to the war," she didn't join the protestors: she was deeply offended by those who chanted against and cursed returning American servicemen. She said later, "My feeling of patriotism was simply too strong to march against my own country."

She tried to forget Vietnam, locking up her "memories with a vengeance, not just the boxes of photographs, letters, and carbons of stories, but my nightmare images of firefights and the battlefield dead and wounded and the insanity of it all."

Working for the Associated Press, Jurate covered the Arab-Israeli War in October 1973 before becoming a White House correspondent during Jimmy Carter's presidency, during which she covered the First Lady's office.

But during "one frantic night," Vietnam came back to Jurate's mind in a powerful way, and she "became obsessed about the fate of the men" she had interviewed during the war. She got in touch with one of Captain Bynum's men, Anthony Benedetto, who had been 20 years old in 1967. He remembered Jurate. "We thought you were crazy to be out there with us," he said.

Jurate asked him about Captain Bynum. How had he died?

Three days after Jurate's evacuation, Anthony said, the patrol had returned to Khe Sanh only to be ordered back out hours later to assist some men enmeshed in a desperate battle. Captain Bynum was hit in the chest and continued fighting, but was rescued too late.

Jurate, it turned out, hadn't been even remotely responsible for his death.

She became a passionate advocate for refugees, seeking US aid for them and personally visiting war-torn Bosnia, Rwanda, Pakistan, and Afghanistan. She received a Freedom Award in 2010 from the International Rescue Committee. She is a board member of the Women's Refugee Commission and currently serves as president of the Kazickas Family Foundation, an educational philanthropic organization focused on her native Lithuania.

Jurate lives in New York City.

LEARN MORE

Odyssey of Hope by Joseph Kazickas (Tyto Alba, 2006).
A memoir by Jurate's father, detailing his family's escape from Communist-controlled Lithuania and their years as refugees in Germany and life in the New World.

On Their Own: Women Journalists and the American Experience in Vietnam by Joyce Hoffmann (Da Capo, 2008).

"These Hills Called Khe Sanh" by Jurate Kazickas, in *War Torn: Stories of War from the Women Reporters Who Covered Vietnam* by Tad Bartimus et al. (Random House, 2002).

IRIS MARY ROSER

Australian Relief Worker

IRIS MARY ROSER HAD A LONG history of war-related relief work. As a teenager during World War II, she had delivered groceries—filling in for delivery men who had been called to active duty—in Tenterfield, her hometown in the Australian state of New South Wales, before she joined the Australian Women's Land Army, working on farms to help prevent a famine.

Iris Mary married shortly after the war, and while raising three sons, she also found time to serve in numerous charities. But in 1967 she and her husband began having marital trouble and divorced. Now she needed a new start. But what would it be?

Australia was sending troops and medical teams to Vietnam, so the war was constantly in the news. One day Iris Mary read a newspaper article about an organization called Project Concern (PC), which was running a hospital in an area of South Vietnam known as the Central Highlands. The PC hospital and clinic desperately needed volunteers. Iris Mary immediately knew that she must be one of them and signed up to go. But as she

Iris Mary in 1968. *Iris Mary Roser,* Ba Rose: My Years in Vietnam, 1968–1971 *(Sydney: Pan Books, 1991)*

prepared to leave, she had to fight off intense waves of fear: she had never traveled very far from her hometown.

If she had been afraid before her journey began, those fears were significantly increased when Iris Mary reached Hong Kong by ocean liner. Chilling news was coming out of Vietnam: Communist fighters had successfully mounted a surprise attack on more than 100 South Vietnamese towns and cities during the Tet holiday.

All flights to Saigon were canceled for the next 16 days. Finally, on February 18, 1968, Iris Mary flew out of Hong Kong and landed in Saigon.

It was a war zone. "I walked off the plane to find myself surrounded by mayhem," Iris Mary wrote later. "Artillery was booming nearby; tanks and reams of barbed wire were everywhere; weapon-laden soldiers were hurrying in all directions."

After several misunderstandings and misdirections, Iris Mary arrived at the Dalat US military base, which was on high alert for enemy activity. When she requested a ride to the PC hospital, located 25 miles away outside the village of Dam Pao, the base commander seemed shocked. And irritated.

"Don't you know there's a war going on out there, ma'am?" he asked.

But another man standing nearby told Iris Mary that an armed helicopter, or gunship, was headed for that area in order to sweep with gunfire, or strafe, a Vietcong (VC)–occupied village. He suggested she come along. He would drop her off afterward, he said.

Iris Mary was placed between two machine gunners. "But unlike them, I did not have ear muffs," she wrote later, "and when the village was underneath us and the firepower started I thought my eardrums would explode as their guns spat bullets by the hundreds."

Shortly afterward, the hospital came into sight. By the time the gunship dropped her off, Iris Mary's legs were shaking so much she wondered if they would hold her up. They did, and the staff greeted her eagerly. A young woman named Tuyet, who came forward to help Iris Mary with her luggage, said, "Unfortunately, you have arrived at a time of sadness and tension. Many of the villages around us have been attacked. Relatives of some of the staff have been killed, the homes of others have been destroyed. We are all afraid that the hospital will be next."

An American nurse took Iris Mary on a tour of the hospital and clinic. Everything was shockingly rudimentary, and each hospital bed contained two patients. Others lay on the floor.

All but four of the staff members were Montagnards (French for "mountain dwellers"), people who were native to the Central Highlands. Because the war had forced many of the area's Montagnards out of their homes, they had become nomads, staying wherever they could grow some rice and live in relative safety.

Iris Mary drove weekly to the more advanced hospital in Dalat. There she collected food and medical supplies for the Dam Pao PC clinic and hospital. Sometimes she took patients to Dalat if their medical issues were too complex for the PC hospital.

Although Dam Pao was in the midst of a VC-controlled area, the PC workers had been told "through the village news network" that they could use the roads between 8:00 AM and 3:00 PM. The staff all knew why: Project Concern was a nonpolitical organization. As such, it asked no questions and treated all medical issues, including battle wounds, and all patients, including VC fighters.

But the VC were determined to assert their authority, often in terrifying ways. One day, while Iris Mary and a young Montagnard PC staff member named K'Duc were driving back from the Dalat hospital after dropping off a patient, they saw, in the middle of the road, the body of a dead man. Iris Mary immediately stopped, wanting to cover it somehow before any children saw it.

K'Duc grabbed her before she could get out. "Go! Go!" he yelled.

When they arrived back at the clinic, K'Duc told her that the VC had killed the man and displayed his body in order to keep the local people in line.

But the PC team members continued their work. Whenever there was a lull in fighting, they traveled through neighboring villages instead of waiting for the villagers to come to the clinic. They would always begin by greeting the headman and the medicine man. Then Iris Mary assisted the medics as they treated a variety of ailments: malaria, intestinal parasites, tuberculosis, respiratory infections, abscesses, chicken pox, mumps, measles.

Many of the village people lived in constant pain. "Their gratitude for a handful of aspirin was heart-rending," Iris Mary remembered. "Our medics won my utmost admiration as they gently treated the people. They were not only giving a little relief from suffering, but also showing that the people at the PC hospital really cared."

One day a group of particularly sick people walked into the hospital from Durbrach, a village about six miles away. Their festering lumps and high fevers were diagnosed as bubonic plague, and someone at the hospital made an urgent call to the province office at Thu Duc to request extra vaccines.

Iris Mary and K'Krai, a Montagnard PC staff member, drove to Durbrach to convince the other villagers to get vaccinated. But when they arrived, the village was deserted. Strings with meat hung in every doorway. K'Krai explained why: the villagers had attempted "to appease their gods" before fleeing into the jungle. Iris Mary and K'Krai were certain that many of the villagers were already infected and would die if not vaccinated.

Province officials, through the use of a helicopter and a loudspeaker, urged the Durbrach villagers to come to the hospital for their vaccinations.

Infected villagers heard the message and came by the hundreds for their first of two injections. But a few days later, when the villagers tried to return for the second shot, the roads around the hospital were blocked. Although the barriers were only sawed-off trees, everyone knew the VC had put them there. So the villagers stayed away.

These roadblocks also caused food shortages for the hospital staff. When the staff's supply was down to one bag of rice, Iris Mary decided to visit a farmer who always sold his vegetables to the PC for a nominal price. A PC worker named Phu accompanied Iris Mary on the drive, breaking the tension and making her laugh. "Hello, Mrs. Water Buffalo," he would say to any buffalo they passed. "You are looking well today. Have you seen any naughty men with guns? Miss Buffalo, how sweet you look. Could you tell us if there are any 'Charlies' [Vietcong] around?"

They made it to the farm, loaded the vehicle with vegetables, then returned without a single VC encounter.

VICTOR CHARLIE AND THE VIETCONG

The NATO phonetic alphabet, created in the 1950s, assigns a word for every letter of the English alphabet in order to avoid confusion during radio communications. The words help differentiate letters that might sound similar when spoken, such as *M* and *N*, or *P* and *V*. The word assigned to *V* is *Victor* and to *C* is *Charlie*. So when discussing the Vietcong during radio communications, instead of saying "VC," military personnel used the code "Victor Charlie."

But the VC remained active in the area, always exerting their control. One day a young girl was brought into the clinic with knife marks crisscrossed all over her body. This had been done, the medics were told, to punish her mother, who had made the mistake of selling rice to an Army of the Republic of Vietnam (ARVN) soldier.

The VC fighters would also set themselves up as tax collectors at checkpoints, stopping vehicles and charging each driver a fee. Whenever Iris Mary drove through the checkpoints, however, she was never stopped. Though she tried to play it cool, she was actually terrified when driving through these areas, writing later that she was always "expecting a burst of gunfire into the tyres that thankfully never came."

One day the headman from Sre Rung, a nearby Montagnard village, came by PC asking if the workers would obtain some rice from Dalat and store it at the hospital and clinic for his village's people.

Months before, the VC had occupied Sre Rung, living in tunnels and bunkers underneath the homes. When the VC guerrillas demanded a share of the village's rice supply, there wasn't enough left for the villagers.

The PC staff agreed, and the plan worked—until the VC discovered it. When the VC retaliated by destroying village property, the elders decided to move their village elsewhere.

The Southern government provided the villagers temporary protective quarters in the form of iron sheds near the hospital. Iris Mary was amazed at how quietly and courageously these Montagnards—1,000 men, women, and children—left their homes one day and found spots for themselves inside the sheds. That night the government bombed their village to destroy the VC bunkers.

A relatively peaceful period followed. The PC staff began to joke that "Charlie" had taken a holiday. But then one day at 2:00 PM, while she rested on the porch during the siesta, Iris Mary heard "a hiss." She looked around the corner of the building and saw "a dark head and beckoning finger." The stranger had come to give a message: the VC were on their way to attack a village only about 500 yards from the PC hospital, which would be next. The first attack was planned that day for 5:00 PM.

Iris Mary quickly relayed the message to the hospital staff and villagers, and the villagers immediately began evacuating on foot. Iris Mary and the doctors knew they could call for helicopter evacuation. But as their Montagnard staff wouldn't be included in the evacuation, they chose to remain.

Their situation was desperate. The hospital's jeep and the ambulance were in Dalat being repaired. An old ambulance was nearby, but its driver, Ong Krah, was using it to collect wood, as he always did on his day off. If he didn't return on time, they would have to walk.

Despite the tension, no one panicked as they packed their bags. The villagers walked by: adults carrying bundles taller than themselves, children carrying younger children, old people riding in carts.

By 4:30 the stream of villagers was thinning. One of the workers began to weep. Then another cried out, "Ong Krah, he is coming!"

With only seven minutes to spare, the PC staff drove away.

Iris Mary decided to stay at the US base in Lien Hiep, where she could keep informed about VC activities in Dam Pao. The rest of the staff stayed at the Cam Do Hotel while they visited the surrounding villages.

About a week after the scheduled VC attack on the hospital, Iris Mary asked the US colonel in charge if the staff could return.

"I wondered how long it would be before you asked that question," he said. "Are you sure you want to go back?"

"Yes, of course."

"You had problems getting out, you may not make it next time."

Iris Mary insisted. He refused at first but finally relented, though not before voicing his doubts about the rest of the team's courage. "How stupid can you be to expect them to volunteer to go back in there?" he asked. "They would have to be as crazy as you are."

Apparently they were. The others arrived to pick up Iris in a military vehicle filled with supplies, ready to return to Dam Pao.

On their return, they discovered that the VC had only taken food and drugs; the hospital equipment remained untouched.

As much as she had enjoyed her work with Project Concern, Iris Mary decided not to renew her contract with them. In November 1968 she began working for a different organization in Vietnam called Civil Operations and Rural Development Support, or CORDS. They didn't have a specific job for Iris Mary, but when they saw her excellent references from PC, they decided to create a new position: social welfare adviser for Gia Dinh Province. She accepted the position, became "Ba [Mrs.] Rose" to the other CORDS employees, and took an apartment in Saigon.

The Southern government and the United States had created CORDS to inspire loyalty among Southern civilians. But some of Iris Mary's duties—inspecting welfare institutions and following through on all requests for social welfare—opened her eyes to the blatant corruption that was rampant in the Southern government.

Her first assignment brought her to a province office where she was to sign receipts for rice to be distributed to refugees. The form stated there were 20 units of rice, but Iris wouldn't sign for something she hadn't checked. When she did check, she discovered there were only 16 units of rice.

"Who are the recipients of the other four?" she asked the CORDS representative who had accompanied her.

He shrugged.

"I'll go and find out for myself at the depot at Can Tho," she said.

"No! No!" he cried. "You must not do that, Ba Rose. You would not get back to Gia Dinh alive."

Iris Mary had a sudden, chilling realization that "danger in Vietnam did not just come from the Vietcong"—she might be killed by officials of the very government she was working for!

When she complained to the province chief, he replied, very calmly, that she had to accept the situation: "If you want to work in harmony with Vietnamese officials, you must learn to do things the Vietnamese way."

Iris Mary was thoroughly disgusted that in order to do her job, she had to become "a link in a chain of corruption." And soon she found corruption in a far more disturbing place: an orphanage.

An Trong was an unregistered orphanage managed by an overly friendly woman whose hands flashed with diamond rings but who didn't seem to know specific details about the children under her care.

Iris Mary went to check on the orphanage and meet with the children. While playing with a group of them, she heard whimpering from behind a closed door with a cot jammed against it. She moved the cot and opened the door. On the other side was a small girl lying in her own waste.

When Iris Mary asked the manger for means to clean the girl, the obviously embarrassed woman claimed she was not at fault.

An Trong orphans. Iris Mary is standing in back, at center. *Iris Mary Roser,* Ba Rose: My Years in Vietnam, 1968–1971 *(Sydney: Pan Books, 1991)*

The girl's mother, she said, had left her and never returned. The girl refused to eat.

A doctor diagnosed the girl with malnutrition. Iris named the girl Small One and hired a caregiver to watch Small One in her apartment.

Small One improved in a few weeks, but she never smiled or even cried. When she wasn't sleeping, she only stared or whimpered.

A few weeks later a young American in civilian clothes named John Roberts came to Iris Mary's CORDS office. He had been searching for a little girl, he said, the daughter of the Vietnamese interpreter of his former unit. He had promised to take care of his friend's daughter if anything should happen.

When his friend was killed, John attempted to search for the girl, but the Vietnamese authorities stood in his way. He tried to extend his tour in order to search for her, but the US military wouldn't allow it. Upon his return to the United States, he sent money to the girl's mother, but she never acknowledged receipt of it. Deeply worried, he returned to Vietnam.

John then located the girl's mother only to learn that she had brought her daughter to the An Trong orphanage because the child fretted and whimpered all day, missing her father and John. The An Trong manager reluctantly gave John directions to Iris Mary's office, and now here he was. Iris Mary sensed he was telling the truth, so she took John to see Small One.

"When we entered the room, the little girl was lying on her back just staring into space. John walked over and looking down into those big solemn brown eyes spoke gently to her. Ever so slowly, her face lit up with the most beautiful smile," Iris Mary wrote later.

John took Small One away, and Iris Mary never saw them again. Shortly after this happy reunion, the orphanage manager came to visit Iris Mary and frantically offered one of her diamond rings. "She was afraid she would lose her recently gained [government] support, and I assured her this would not happen on the proviso that she advise us in future if she needed help with a sick child," Iris Mary wrote later.

The corruption Iris Mary encountered in her CORDS job continued to sicken her, especially people running orphanages who helped themselves to donations meant for the children in their care. But she continued to try to make a difference, staying in Vietnam until the end of 1971.

Before she left, she received a letter of commendation from Brigadier General James A. Herbert, deputy acting commissioner of CORDS, which stated, in part: "In sum, here is a totally honest, courageous, perceptive, gracious, tough, understanding and tender lady. She has been of great service to the Vietnamese 'little' people and a great help to the US Mission in the field of Social Welfare Assistance. Her departure will be a great loss; her splendid efforts will be remembered."

After leaving Vietnam, Iris Mary worked in Australia as director of several geriatric care facilities, then as the coordinator of a family shelter, before working for one year in an Indian leper colony. When she retired, Iris Mary became a volunteer welfare worker for the Salvation Army.

LEARN MORE

Ba Rose: My Years in Vietnam, 1968–1971 by Iris Mary Roser (Pan Books, 1991).

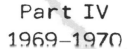

Part IV
1969–1970

RICHARD M. NIXON'S "PEACE"

★

WHEN RICHARD M. NIXON was inaugurated as president of the United States on January 20, 1969, the majority of Americans considered the US involvement in Vietnam to have been a mistake. But these same Americans were divided on how to end that involvement. Some thought the United States should immediately pull out of Vietnam, whereas others felt that doing so would harm America's international reputation and that the United States should strive for some sort of decisive victory to bolster its image.

The new president was definitely in the latter category. Since the 1950s, while serving as Dwight D. Eisenhower's vice president, Nixon had spoken out repeatedly about America's need to defeat the international spread of Communism, implying that if the United States lost Vietnam to Ho Chi Minh, all of Southeast Asia would soon follow, eventually igniting a third World War. Indeed, Nixon's anticommunist rhetoric had been partly responsible for creating a climate in which politicians, including Democrat presidents John F. Kennedy and Lyndon B. Johnson, feared being perceived as weak on this issue (especially since a Democrat president, Harry Truman, had been in office in 1949 when China had fallen to the Communists).

But now, in 1969, on the verge of a new decade, the United States was still fighting an old war with which Americans had grown weary. Nixon knew this, and so the president was planning to show two faces. To his public, he would be the peace-loving leader who, later in the year, would begin to fulfill his promise to bring the US troops home from Vietnam.

His other face would be that of a madman.

Nixon was convinced that the only honorable way the United States could leave Vietnam was by first ensuring a stable South Vietnamese government capable of defending itself from the Communist North. And the only way that the Northern Hanoi government would give up, Nixon thought, would be if it was somehow defeated in a decisive military victory. Or perhaps through diplomatic threats.

Henry Kissinger, Nixon's secretary of state, was in Paris attempting to negotiate a peace settlement between representatives of the Vietnamese Communists and those of the Southern government. The talks, like the war itself, were in a stalemate, with accusations flowing as freely as the French wine provided for the diplomats' luncheons.

To speed things up, Nixon directed Kissinger to promote the "madman theory." Kissinger was to imply, in private conversations with the Communist delegates, that the US president was so determined to win the war on his own terms there was no predicting how he might attempt to do so, including the use of nuclear weapons.

But how to make the Communists believe the madman theory? In March, Nixon ordered the secret bombing of sanctuaries that the North Vietnamese Army (NVA) and Vietcong (VC) were using inside Cambodia's border. These sanctuaries had been a boon to the Communist fighters but a thorn in the side of the American troops because they weren't allowed to pursue their enemies into the officially neutral country.

Nixon hoped the madman theory would have a quick effect, for he knew he had only months before news of the secret bombings leaked. When it did, there would certainly be backlash from American antiwar protestors. But even in this, the president had time: following the previous year's Democratic National Convention, which had erupted into riots between protestors and police, most middle-class Americans had a low opinion of antiwar protestors.

Then two different major news stories came out that gave Americans an even lower opinion of the war. On May 10 the Battle of Hill 937 began one mile east of the Laotian border when a search-and-destroy mission encountered an NVA stronghold on Ap Bia Mountain. The struggle for control of the mountain lasted 10 days. Because the fierce fighting resulted in hundreds of dead and wounded on both sides, the US media called the event the Battle of Hamburger Hill.

Shortly after the Americans had driven out the North Vietnamese, they were ordered to abandon the site. The NVA moved right back in.

When the popular *Life* magazine published an issue the following month showing on its cover the smiling faces of 241 young Americans killed within one week in Vietnam, many American readers mistakenly assumed that all 241 had been on Hill 937 (whereas 5 of the 56 Americans killed there actually appeared in the photograph).

For many Americans, the Battle of Hamburger Hill—which would be the last major search-and-destroy mission US troops conducted—became a symbol of the war's futility.

Then in November 1969, the Associated Press broke a harrowing story: a company of US soldiers had slaughtered approximately 500 unarmed South Vietnamese civilians (many of whom they raped before killing them) in the My Lai hamlet. What made the My Lai Massacre particularly disturbing was not only the calm nonchalance with which it had been conducted—one witness reported that the soldiers took a lunch break during the murders—but also that the US military had covered up the atrocity for more than a year: the killings had occurred in March 1968.

Antiwar activists, energized by the Hamburger Hill and My Lai Massacre stories, began to organize nationwide antiwar activities that average Americans could embrace, such as candlelight vigils and special church services. During one particularly powerful protest, people carrying signs, each with the name of one fighting man killed in Vietnam, walked single-file from Arlington National Cemetery past the White House and, one by one, placed the signs in a large coffin.

The success of these protest events made Nixon realize the increasing difficulty of leading the country while maintaining open escalation in the war. And he knew the Hanoi government was aware of American protests. Indeed, Hanoi media outlets often published public letters supporting American antiwar protestors. So in Nixon's continued determination to win the war on his terms, on November 3, 1969, he gave his "Silent Majority" speech, proving to the people of Hanoi—and the United States—that he would not be moved. In his lengthy speech, detailing the history of the war and his plans to end it, Nixon claimed that even now, most Americans, whom he called "the great silent majority of my fellow Americans," were willing to end the war in the right way—that is, his way—even if it took more time.

The right way, he said in the same speech, would include something called Vietnamization: the forces of South Vietnam would assume more responsibility for their defense as the American fighting men were gradually phased out. "The defense of freedom is everybody's business, not just America's business," the president said. "And it is particularly the responsibility of the people whose freedom is threatened. In the previous administration, we Americanized the war in Vietnam. In this administration, we are Vietnamizing the search for peace."

But in the beginning of 1970 the peace talks were again at a stalemate. Nixon decided to make a bold move to bring the North Vietnamese diplomats back to the bargaining table. On April 30, 1970, he ordered the ground invasion of Cambodia. This expansion of the war was no secret. He told the American people, in a speech broadcast over radio and television, of his plan to invade Cambodia "for the purpose of ending the war in Vietnam."

The American people wanted none of it. Congress immediately moved to severely limit Nixon's ability to wage war. And protests erupted on college campuses nationwide. On May 4, 1970, after students at Kent State University in Ohio set fire to an Army Reserve Officers' Training Corps building, the Ohio National Guard was called in, and they fired into a crowd of unarmed student protestors. Four students were killed and nine wounded. One was paralyzed for life.

American frustration with the Vietnam War had reached new heights and the president's approval rating a new low. Nixon turned his sights to his 1972 reelection, all the while stewing about the failure, in his opinion, of the American people to help him win the war.

To take people's minds off the war, he began to concentrate on improving relations with the Soviet Union and China, claiming in a televised address that America "might be on the threshold of a generation of peace."

Because both China and the Soviet Union were supporters of North Vietnam's war against America and South Vietnam, Hanoi officials were quite alarmed at this possible thawing between the United States and its Cold War enemies. Indeed, North Vietnam's allies were nearly as weary of the war as Americans were.

But it was far from over.

ANNE KOCH

"I Knew in My Heart That I Had to Go"

ANNE KOCH WAS RAISED BY two World War II veterans. Her father, George Koch, had been severely wounded while on a reconnaissance mission searching for Erwin Rommel, the commander of the German army in North Africa.

After receiving immediate care, George was sent back to the United States via transport ship and admitted to the Walter Reed army hospital in Washington, DC. There he fell in love with the head nurse on the chest surgery floor, a woman named Helen Adams. They were married on June 4, 1944.

George and Helen were determined to instill patriotism and an understanding of American history in their children. So the Koch family spent many summer vacations visiting sites of historic American battles—such as Lexington and Concord, in Massachusetts, and Valley Forge and Gettysburg, in Pennsylvania—as well as Independence Hall and the Liberty Bell, in Philadelphia.

In middle school, Anne's teachers often showed vocational films in class. One such film showed doctors at work. The girls

Anne at the Tomb of the Unknown Soldier, South Vietnam. *Anne Koch Voigt*

in the class began screaming, "Ooh, blood!" Anne, however, found the film quite fascinating. In fact, from that moment on, she was determined to follow in her mother's footsteps, and in 1966 she graduated from the Chester County Hospital School for Nursing.

Anne was working there on the men's ward when an army nurse recruiter and her sergeant came to speak about the need for army nurses. Anne gave them her name and information.

But her grandmother died shortly afterward, so Anne delayed her decision on whether to enter basic training. The army nurse in charge of recruits then gave Anne an ultimatum: either come to the July 1968 basic training at Fort Sam Houston, in San Antonio, Texas, or forget the whole thing. Anne's sense of duty to her country kicked in, and she went.

After basic training, she was ordered to San Francisco, where she worked for several months in a ward of Vietnam veterans, all amputees. "It was quite a shock!" Anne admits now. Her greatest challenge was projecting a calm demeanor as she watched these young men struggle with new prosthetic limbs, relearning how to do simple things such as walk or feed themselves.

When Anne turned 23 she received orders to report to Vietnam. And after spending Christmas at home in Pennsylvania, she boarded a plane on December 28, 1968, for the first leg of her trip.

As her parents waved good-bye at the Philadelphia International Airport, tears streamed down their cheeks. It was the first time Anne had seen them crying together, and it moved her powerfully. But her sense of duty was strong, and she kept walking, saying later of that moment, "I knew in my heart that I had to go."

After stops in San Francisco, Alaska, and Japan, Anne finally landed in Vietnam in the middle of the night. "I don't know why I thought it would be a normal landing," she said, but she was surprised at just how utterly abnormal it was. To avoid the plane becoming an enemy target, "the lights went on inside, they went off, they came on, and then off." And the landing was abrupt, "the fastest I've ever landed in my life," Anne describes. "Boom, we were down."

When the chief nurse in charge of all American nurses in Vietnam gave Anne a choice of working in either the 2nd Surgical Hospital or the 93rd Evacuation Hospital in Long Binh, Anne chose the evacuation hospital; she had promised her father that if given a choice, she would work in the most secure location, and the surgical hospital was in a more dangerous area.

Anne went to work in ward 3, a surgical ICU and recovery unit with 35 beds for intensive care patients and 15 for those who were recovering. When she arrived, all the beds were filled. And she learned that she was replacing a nurse whose husband had just been killed and who was now on her way home with his body.

Most of the 93rd Evacuation Hospital's buildings had been structured in the shape of a cross. This was deliberate; if one portion was hit by enemy artillery, the entire building would not be destroyed.

On ward 3, the left side of the cross, section A held patients with chest wounds, and section B, the top of the cross, was for those with abdominal wounds. The right side of the cross,

The 93rd Evacuation Hospital at Long Binh. Ward 3 is located at the back of the center row. *Anne Koch Voigt*

section C, was for burn and amputee cases, and the bottom of the cross, section D, was for those in recovery. The nurse's station was located in the center of the cross and consisted of two desks pushed together and a podium holding an enormous log book with each patient's name, rank, unit, and medical facts.

The critically ill patients were always near the nurse's station, but most patients stayed for only three days. Like most evacuation hospitals, the 93rd was the first place seriously wounded men were taken straight out of combat. As soon as they were stable enough to endure transportation, they were moved to Saigon for more involved treatment before being flown to Japan and finally to the United States.

During their long shifts, the nurses in ward 3 were constantly on their feet, checking on their patients and monitoring their treatment equipment: IV drips, chest tubes, suction machines, breathing tubes, and stomach tubes and dressings. The burn cases, which were quite common at the 93rd, were the most difficult to care for. In American hospitals burn patients were soaked in large water-filled tubs called Hubbard tanks, the least painful way to treat severe burns. In Vietnam there wasn't enough water pressure to fill such a tank. So instead Anne and the other nurses could only give their burn patients heavy pain medications like morphine before washing their skin and applying healing ointment. This process was excruciatingly painful, no matter how light a nurse's touch.

Because their wounds were so painful, burn patients could sometimes become seriously confused. As Anne was applying cream to one young soldier's burns, he suddenly jumped out of bed and towered over her. Anne thought that, in his delirium, he might harm her; in spite of his injuries, he was still very strong.

But the other nurses came to Anne's rescue, and together they put the young soldier back into his bed.

"KEEP THE FAITH"

A medic wrote this poem for Anne on April 5, 1969. After receiving it, she wrote the words KEEP THE FAITH on the back of her hat.

"A Poem for Anne Koch"
Here we are in Vietnam
Twelve months to go
Most of us leave with a lot,
Or nothing to show.
No matter what your job is,
No matter your chore,
It will prey on your mind
By outlook, less or more
Until the day we leave this
God-awful land,
Keep the faith, Baby
And meet the demand.

Anne and the other nurses realized that the men sometimes saw them as surrogates for the women in their lives: wives, mothers, girlfriends. So they tried to care for their patients' emotional needs as well as their medical ones. "We would smile and listen as much as we could," Anne says.

One day Anne had an unforgettable conversation with a wounded soldier that highlighted the tremendous difficulties of the war from the American point of view. This young soldier had been on a long-range reconnaissance patrol in a jungle when he encountered two young men whose appearance and behavior made him certain they were Vietcong recruits. He shot and killed them before they could kill him.

But he discovered later that they were just two boys who had been playing, pretending to be soldiers at war, he described it as "Cowboys and Indians, Vietnam style." The American soldier couldn't cope with his overwhelming guilt. Anne tried to comfort him, telling him that it could have happened to anyone. "War is not always black and white," she said. Mistakes, like the one he'd made, "can happen in the twinkling of an eye."

Another of Anne's patients suffered from survivor's guilt after a mission with his long-range reconnaissance patrol unit. The Americans were on a trail when they saw North Vietnamese Army (NVA) soldiers headed their way. The Americans hid while the NVA soldiers approached with their water buffalo. When the animal stopped and turned its head toward the hidden Americans, apparently sensing their presence, the NVA soldiers opened fire on the hidden unit, killing every American except

---

EXCERPT FROM A LETTER TO ANNE KOCH VOIGHT FROM AIR CAVALRY SERGEANT ROBERT McCANCE:

I never forgot the care you gave me those many years ago. I never forgot your name I guess cause you were so kind to me at a time when I really needed the touch of a mother's hand. I really never gave your plight, that of a nurse in a combat zone, much thought until I watched a TV documentary several years ago concerning combat nurses and the emotional trauma you people were experiencing every day. I never realized the scars we left not on you but in you.

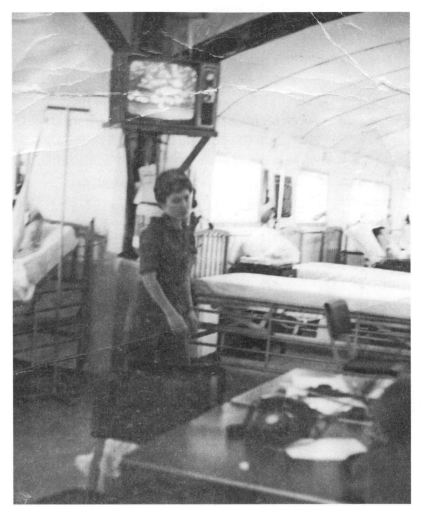

Anne near the nurse's station. *Anne Koch Voigt*

Anne's patient. Anne tried to tell him that the other deaths were not his fault: "There was nothing different you could have done."

The bulk of her time was, of course, devoted to saving lives. One day she was standing at the nurse's desk within view of the bed of a severely wounded helicopter pilot who had been shot down. His femoral artery—the large, deep artery in the thigh—had already been repaired once. When Anne glanced in his direction, she saw that his sheets were turning bright red. His femoral artery had ruptured again!

She raced to his bed, pressed her hand on the ruptured artery, and yelled for help. The pilot was rushed to the ICU and immediately given 8–10 pints of blood, 8–10 more in the operating room while surgeons worked to repair his artery, and then the same amount when he returned to the ICU. After he had stabilized and was put on a plane for Japan, the doctor that accompanied him brought along five more pints of "just-in-case blood." Anne always wondered if he survived.

Blood transfusions saved many lives in Vietnam. In fact, having blood on hand was so crucial that when young American fighting men first arrived in Vietnam, many were immediately brought to the 93rd Evacuation Hospital to donate blood.

Anne could see that this terrified many of these "wide-eyed" recruits; having to donate blood immediately upon landing obviously made these already nervous young men even more so. It was a stark reminder that they also might soon be wounded—or worse. "I knew they were scared and worried," recalls Anne. So to keep them from excessive alarm, the medical personnel made certain that the donations occurred in the back of the hospital, as far away as possible from the patients.

Although a doctor's order was generally necessary to begin a blood transfusion, the nurses had standing orders to do so on their own in emergency situations. Once Anne was caring for a patient whose bandages needed constant changing because his multiple wounds were leaking too much plasma. He asked Anne for a pain shot. "Soon he became white and was starting to go into shock," Anne recalls. "Right at that time, his blood work came back showing he needed blood."

Anne quickly gave him one pint of blood, "which did the trick." He stabilized. Then she went to the head nurse and told her what had happened. The head nurse rechecked his blood level. It was still low. She gave him one more unit.

When a new doctor learned that these nurses had taken it upon themselves to give blood transfusions without waiting for his orders, he was "shocked and upset." He didn't initially realize that this particular situation had been life-threatening or that the nurses had long been coping with similarly serious situations, often on their own, without a doctor's assistance or orders.

By the end of December 1969, it was time for Anne to leave. She had, like most nurses in Vietnam, a "short-time calendar,"

Anne receiving an Army Commendation Medal for meritorious service in the surgical intensive care unit, shortly before leaving Vietnam.
Anne Koch Voigt

precisely tracking their remaining days of service. On her second-to-last day, her superior officer unexpectedly called to tell Anne she was leaving a day early. Because she was caught off guard, Anne didn't get a chance to say good bye to all her friends. Some of them she never saw again. "I had the wrong assumption that somehow I would be able to find them all back in the United States," she says.

Anne's homeward trip took her to Hawaii, California, and finally Philadelphia. Dressed in her "Class As" green army uniform, she turned a corner in the Philadelphia International Airport and came face-to-face with her first representatives of prejudice against Vietnam veterans: a mother and daughter, perfect strangers to Anne, who gave her "the ugliest looks." Anne wanted to say to them, "I haven't done anything wrong. For a year I've worked as hard as I could taking care of wounded GIs; 12 hour shifts, 6 days per week."

But Anne was shy and didn't say a word, not to these two, nor to the many who would follow them. During the postwar years, while Anne worked several different nursing jobs, she was frequently asked bizarre questions and had to endure insinuating comments that stemmed from sweepingly erroneous perceptions about Vietnam veterans in general and Vietnam nurses in particular.

Anne tried not to dwell on these people with their mistaken notions, but her mind did often return to her wounded patients in Vietnam. She knew she had done her best at the time, saying later, "You always knew that the person lying there could be your brother, cousin, or friend, and you wanted to get him home in the best shape possible and as soon as possible." But she had no way of knowing who had survived, especially since the nature of the 93rd's work had been to keep the men only for a few days.

One soldier had stayed at the 93rd for over a month, however, and so he—and his unusual name—remained in Anne's memory longer. Larry Sudweeks had received a chest wound so massive he had been put on a ventilator. Many years later, he and Anne reconnected via letters before reuniting in person at the Vietnam Women's Memorial in Washington, DC, on November 11, 2013, Veteran's Day.

Anne had also been in Washington 20 years earlier at the memorial's dedication, and she is glad it has become a place where women veterans of other wars can find a sense of belonging: when she visited the memorial in 2013 she saw American veterans of the Iraq and Afghanistan wars there in addition to those from the Vietnam War. "It may not have started out to be their memorial, but it has become theirs also," she says.

LEARN MORE

"On Veteran's Day, the Women Who Saved Lives in Vietnam Got a Much Deserved Thanks" by Petula Dvorak, *Washington Post*, November 11, 2013, www.washingtonpost.com/local/on-veterans-day-the-women-who-saved-lives-in-vietnam-got-a-much-deserved-thanks/2013/11/11/591c44c0–4b1e-11e3-ac54-aa84301ced81_story.html?utm_term=.cef71404bcb2. This article includes the story of Anne's reunion with Larry Sudweeks.

A Piece of My Heart: The Stories of Twenty-Six Women Who Served in Vietnam by Keith Walker (Presideo, 1985).

Women in Vietnam: The Oral History by Ron Steinman (TV Books, 2000).

DANG THUY TRAM

Communist Field Surgeon

ON JANUARY 1, 1969, Dr. Dang Thuy Tram recorded in her diary the words of Ho Chi Minh, part of a message he had sent to all those fighting for the Communist cause in the South: "This year greater victories are assured at the battlefront. For independence—for freedom. Fight until the Americans leave, fight until the puppets fall. Advance soldiers, compatriots. North and South reunified, no other spring more joyous."

Thuy had thought of little else since December 23, 1966, when she had left her beloved family in Hanoi and begun the arduous, dangerous trek down Ho Chi Minh Trail, the network of roads used to support the Vietcong (VC) in the South.

Three months later, Thuy had arrived in Duc Pho, a district in the south-central Quang Ngai Province. The people of Quang Ngai had been heavily involved with resistance against the French during the First Indochina War and were now fighting the Americans and the Army of the Republic of Vietnam (ARVN) soldiers. Thuy was assigned to work as the chief

Dang Thuy Tram. *Vietnam Women's Museum, Hanoi*

surgeon in a Duc Pho clinic, saving the lives of VC fighters and North Vietnamese Army (NVA) soldiers so that they could return to the fight.

While Thuy derived great satisfaction from her work, several things caused her intense grief. One was her thwarted attempts to be accepted into the Communist party.

Her motives for wanting to join the party were not like those of many people she knew who simply wanted to advance their careers. Thuy believed that being a party member would allow her to serve the Communist cause more effectively. She recorded in her diary what she believed to be the aims of a true Communist: "Our responsibility is to fight for what is right, to fight for righteousness. To win we must strive, think, and sacrifice our personal gains, perhaps even our own lives. . . . I will dedicate my lifelong career to securing the rights of the common man and the success of the Party!"

Why wasn't Thuy allowed into the party? Her parents were educated. Her father was a surgeon who enjoyed Western music, and her mother was a lecturer at the Hanoi College of

Pharmacology. Thuy had studied medicine and also enjoyed reading Vietnamese poetry along with French and Russian literature. To her great frustration and sorrow, her educated background branded her as bourgeois—that is, middle class and materialistic—and therefore unworthy of Communist Party membership.

Thuy's dedicated medical work and obvious devotion to the cause, however, eventually gained the respect of local Communist Party leaders. On September 28, 1968, she was finally accepted, writing in her diary, "My clearest feeling today is that I must struggle to deserve the title of 'communist.'"

Thuy would also struggle to master her emotions. She found it difficult not to befriend the young men who were risking their lives for Vietnam's unity. "I have a physician's responsibilities and should maintain some degree of objectivity," she wrote, "but I cannot keep my professional compassion for my patients from becoming affection. . . . Something ties them to me and makes them feel very close to me." When the men left the clinic, Thuy often felt as if she had lost a family member.

And when she treated the same patients more than once, her attachment to them became even greater. A soldier named Bon came under her care on three separate occasions. Thuy first treated him for a minor leg wound. He was brought to her a second time for a shoulder injury that resulted in a severe loss of blood. Bon was worried that his shoulder might not heal enough to bear the weight of a gun.

It did heal, and after Bon had recovered, Thuy saw him one day from a distance. "Greetings, Doctor!" he cried, waving his healed arm in the air. "My arm is as good as new!"

But on January 9, 1969, Bon was brought once more to the clinic, his clothing soaked with blood. A mine had lacerated his leg. Thuy amputated it, hoping the operation would at least save Bon's life. It didn't.

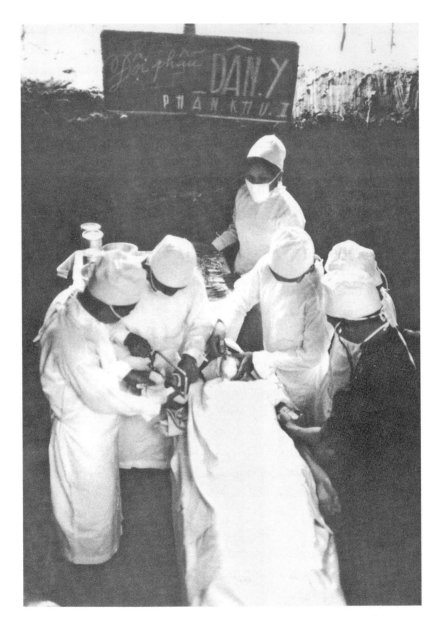

Surgery being performed in a tunnel. *Vietnam Women's Museum, Hanoi*

"Oh, Bon, your blood has crimsoned our native land. . . . Your heart has stopped so that the heart of the nation can beat forever," Thuy wrote in her diary.

She also recorded a very different emotion on this sad occasion, writing, "Hatred for the invaders presses down a thousand times more heavily upon my heart. . . . We will still suffer as long as those bloodthirsty foes remain here."

Two months later, on March 13, Thuy was again saddened by the death of a Communist soldier. She conducted one operation on him, but a second would be necessary to save his life. Although his chances of survival were slim, Thuy wanted to perform the second operation. But she kept this to herself when the rest of the medical team unanimously decided against it. The young man died.

In his pocket, Thuy discovered photos of a girl, a letter promising faithfulness, and a handkerchief embroidered with the words WAITING FOR YOU.

Thuy couldn't get the young man—or his faithful girl-friend—out of her mind. Again she blamed the Americans for this sorrowful loss, describing it as one of the many "crimes committed by the imperialist killers."

At the end of March, she was ordered to report to a different clinic, this one treating both civilian and military cases. The new area, as well as most of the others where Thuy had practiced medicine, were "free-fire zones"; that is, civilians considered friendly to Americans had been evacuated, so the Americans considered anyone remaining to be the enemy and could fire on them without previous orders. This meant that whenever any Americans approached, the clinic personnel had to evacuate. On April 28 Thuy described such an evacuation in her diary:

It's not yet 8:30 a.m., but I urge people to move the injured. I follow them, carrying as many supplies as possible. We trudge up the slope to the school, sweat pouring down our faces, but we dare not pause to rest. . . . Less than an hour and a half later, a barrage of gunshots goes off nearby, so close to us that it seems the enemy has already reached the guard station. I tell all the patients to prepare for another move. We are not ready to do anything, but our terror-stricken highlander guerrilla brothers rush in, saying that the enemy has reached the irrigation gutter. All the local people are fleeing the area.

Thuy was determined not to abandon any wounded. But toward the end, the only people remaining to help evacuate the patients were a few "skinny, sickly teenagers." The Americans were almost upon them. Finally, only one patient remained, a man named Kiem, who had a broken leg. The only medics left in the clinic now were Thuy and a petite female medical student. Thuy ran to get help. Two male medics returned with her, telling her "between ragged breaths" that the Americans had shot one of the wounded soldiers. Then the medics helped Thuy carry Kiem into an underground shelter, where they all hid for an hour until the Americans left the immediate area.

By 4:00 that afternoon, the entire clinic—staff and patients— had arrived safely at their new destination.

But they were never really safe. From April 1969 on, the medics and their wounded were constantly on the move as the increasingly intense fighting grew closer. Each day Thuy could hear "the roar of planes tearing the air" while gunshot volleys rang out day and night.

On May 20 Thuy described another brush with death. Several American HU-1A helicopters, which ARVN soldiers used

Transportation of the wounded in 1968. *Vietnam Women's Museum, Hanoi*

at the time, and a scout plane had circled near the clinic's location. Thuy was very worried by "the intensity of their search."
The area was then hit with exploding grenades, and the house
the medics were using as a patient's ward filled up with smoke.
All the medics and patients rushed into the bunkers under the
house. When the helicopter circled away to begin another pass,
Thuy rushed back up into the house to save any stragglers. No
one was there—all had escaped. She returned to her shelter and
waited out the barrage. It lasted an additional 30 minutes. When
it was over, the staff moved the clinic to a new location.

But the Americans knew that Communists were in the area.
Four days later, Thuy heard an attack of "bombs, bullets, artillery
shells, and airplanes," describing it as "a maelstrom of sounds . . .
usually heard in war movies." On July 16 she described a similar
raid: "Where each bomb strikes, fire and smoke flare up; the

napalm bomb flashes, then explodes in a red ball of fire, leaving dark, thick smoke that climbs into the sky."

During these raids, Thuy always worried about the people she knew and loved. "From a position nearby, I sit with silent fury in my heart," she wrote. "Who is burned in that fire and smoke? In those heaven-shaking explosions, whose bodies are annihilated in the bomb craters? . . . Oh, my heroic people, perhaps no one on earth has suffered more than you."

On July 27 the Americans attacked the hamlet where she was staying. By nightfall, nearly everyone had fled. Thuy walked alone to Pho Quang, a nearby village. It too was deserted. The house she entered was "eerily empty." The village trees had been destroyed. The smell of gunpowder was in the air. The road was pockmarked with craters from artillery.

Thuy finally located a woman, who told her it would be impossible to follow the rest of the villagers, because of enemy shelling. As if to emphasize her point, an artillery explosion suddenly illuminated the pitch-darkness.

This was an unusually dangerous situation for Thuy. Because Communist surgeons were so valuable in the South, they normally traveled with an armed guard who directed their way. Now Thuy had to navigate for herself, and she wasn't sure what to do. "If the enemy comes, where should I run?" she wondered.

While Thuy was confused, she rarely feared for her own safety. After she regrouped with the other medics, she was sent out on a nighttime emergency mission and bravely walked through hostile territory with her guard. "Perhaps I will meet the enemy, and perhaps I will fall, but I hold my medical bag firmly regardless," she wrote in her diary.

She hadn't yet met the Americans face-to-face, but Thuy had definitely heard them from the underground shelters and bunkers, walking, shouting, and searching for their hidden enemies.

When the rainy season began and the underground hideaways filled with water, hiding became increasingly difficult.

Her attempt to stay one step ahead of the Americans soon cast her out of doors, hidden in some bushes, "soaking wet and shivering." Yet she was happy, even at this moment of difficulty, "to be a part of the resistance, to be in this very scene" with her comrades.

On December 31, 1969, Thuy wrote, "Death is close. Just the other day, if I had been a few minutes late, I would have been dead or captured. We started to run when the enemy was less than twenty meters away. Fortunately, no comrade or wounded soldier was lost."

But one day she found the body of a dead comrade on the road. Next to him, in the fresh mud, were the prints of large boots. The road was covered with electrical wires from American mines.

On June 2, 1970, Thuy's new clinic took a direct hit. Five patients were instantly killed, and the surrounding area was devastated. "Trees downed in every direction, houses flattened or knocked askew, tattered clothes blown up in the tree branches," Thuy described.

Ten days later, the Americans attacked the same group of medics at a different location. No one was injured, but it was frighteningly clear someone had betrayed their location. They had to move again.

The evacuation took place on June 14. Left behind were Thuy, three other female medics, and five seriously wounded soldiers too weak to be moved. They were told to wait until an escort came; it was too dangerous for them to even venture outside.

They waited. One of the wounded fighters, a 19-year-old commando, told the women to run if the enemy came. They were down to their last meal, and still they waited.

Finally, help arrived. Thuy, the other medics, and their patients were evacuated safely.

A few days later, Thuy was walking on a trail with a soldier and two other Vietnamese people when she finally came face-to-face with a group of Americans. Her body was later found by some local villagers. She had been shot in the head.

Her diaries fell into the hands of Fred Whitehurst, an American working for military intelligence. Assigned to destroy enemy documents, Fred was about to throw Thuy's diaries in a fire when his Vietnamese interpreter, ARVN sergeant Nguyen Trung Hieu, who had read the diaries, stopped him. "Don't burn this one, Fred," he said. "It has fire in it already."

As Sergeant Hieu read the diaries to Fred evening by evening, Fred was powerfully moved. Although he knew he should have turned them in, he kept them when he left Vietnam in 1972.

In 2005 Fred located Thuy's family and gave them the diaries. Later that year, they were published in Hanoi as one volume, becoming a bestseller. Young Vietnamese people particularly liked the book; they had learned about the war from textbooks and war diaries that described the war in a formal, grandiose style. In contrast, Thuy's diary presented the unpretentious voice of a warm, intelligent, and occasionally self-doubting young person caught up in the horror of war. Older Vietnamese Communists, who perhaps wondered if the long, destructive war had been worth it in the end, were uplifted by this patriotic young woman's words:

> What agony! Must I keep filling my small diary with pages of blood? But, Thuy! Let's record, record completely all the blood and bones, sweat and tears that our compatriots have shed for the last twenty years. And in the last days

WOMEN'S CONTRIBUTIONS TO THE COMMUNIST CAUSE

Vietnamese Communist leaders called the Vietnam War a "struggle for national salvation." As such, every able-bodied person had to be mobilized, women included. An estimated 1.5 million Vietnamese women were involved in some type of active combat during the war, 60,000 of whom were officially part of the Northern Vietnamese Army. The rest fought in local militias or guerrilla units, many participating part-time in this effort because they were still responsible for food production.

Vietnamese women combat veterans received little recognition until 1995, when the Vietnam Women's Museum in Hanoi opened. The museum celebrates women warriors throughout Vietnam's history but places equal emphasis on the traditional female role of motherhood. These two ideals clashed tragically following the Vietnam War when thousands of women veterans were unable to have children: some women had lost their health during the grueling years of combat, and others couldn't find husbands because too many men their age had been killed.

A militia unit armed with World War II–era German machine guns, most likely captured by the Soviet army. *Vietnam Women's Museum, Hanoi*

of this fatal struggle, each sacrifice is even more worthy of accounting, of remembering. Why? Because we have fought and sacrificed for many years; hope has shone like a bright light burning at the end of the road.

In 2007 Thuy's diary was translated into English and published under the title *Last Night I Dreamed of Peace*.

LEARN MORE

Even the Women Must Fight: Memories of War from North Vietnam by Karen Gottschang Turner, with Phan Thanh Hao (John Wiley & Sons, 1998).

Last Night I Dreamed of Peace: The Diary of Dang Thuy Tram, translated by Andrew X. Pham (Harmony Books, 2007).

Patriots: The Vietnam War Remembered from All Sides by Christian G. Appy (Penguin Books, 2004).

Portrait of the Enemy: The Other Side of Vietnam, Told Through Interviews with North Vietnamese, Former Vietcong, and Southern Opposition Leaders by David Chanoff and Doan Van Toai (Random House, 1986).

LYNDA VAN DEVANTER

"Why Do They Have to Die?"

LYNDA VAN DEVANTER WAS in her last year of nursing school in Baltimore, Maryland, when the war in Vietnam began to press into her consciousness.

"Those guys look so young," she said one night to her roommate, Barbara, as the two watched the news about the war.

"Most of them are no more than eighteen or nineteen," Barbara said.

Lynda began to research the war. She read that the United States was attempting to save South Vietnam from a Communist takeover by the North. "There were brave boys fighting and dying for democracy, and if our boys were being blown apart, then somebody better be over there putting them back together again," she wrote later. "I started to think that maybe that somebody should be me."

So when an army recruiter came to the nursing school in January 1968, both Lynda and Barbara were ready to sign up.

"Are you crazy?" asked Gina, their friend and fellow nursing student. "You go in the Army, they'll send you to Vietnam. It's dangerous over there."

"I want to go to Vietnam," answered Lynda simply.

"But what if you get killed?" Gina asked.

"The sergeant told us that nurses don't get killed," Barbara said. "They're all in rear areas. The hospitals are perfectly safe."

"I think you're both nuts," Gina said. "Leave the wars to the men."

They ignored her advice, and after graduation Lynda and Barbara drove off to Fort Sam Houston, Texas, for their basic training. One activity they practiced repeatedly in training was what to do in a "mass-cal" (mass casualty) situation, when the hospital would be suddenly overwhelmed with wounded men.

During a mass-cal, the nurses would have to use something called triage. They would quickly assess each wounded man, then take one of three actions: (1) send him immediately to surgery; (2) have him wait his turn for surgery; or (3) ease his pain before allowing the inevitable to happen.

"Essentially, we were deciding who would live and who would die," Lynda wrote later. It was a difficult concept for her since she had become a nurse to save lives. But her instructors made it clear that if precious time was spent on one hopeless case, those with survivable wounds might lose their chances.

On June 8, 1969, 1st Lieutenant Sharon Lane, a 26-year-old nurse from Ohio, became the first (and only) US Army nurse killed in Vietnam as a direct result of enemy fire. She had been sitting on a bed in her hooch—living quarters—when a VC rocket exploded nearby, sending shrapnel in every direction.

A few hours after Sharon's death, the plane carrying Lynda and 350 men began its descent into South Vietnam. When the plane began "jerking wildly," luggage fell from the overhead racks. Terrified, Lynda looked out the window. She could see explosions.

"Men," said the voice of the pilot over the intercom, "we just came into a little old firefight back there and it looks like them V.C. ain't taking too kindly to us droppin' in on Tan Son Nhut. So we're gonna take a little ride on over to Long Binh and see if we can't get us a more hospitable welcome. Keep your seatbelts buckled and we'll be down faster than you can say Vietnam sucks."

Lynda was slightly reassured by his casual manner and then by their smooth landing in Long Binh. "But if there had ever been any cockiness in me before this trip began, there sure wasn't any now," she wrote later. "In its place was a cold, hard realization: I could die here."

She spent the next few days at the 90th Replacement Detachment at Long Binh. Describing the area later, Lynda wrote, "Coiled barbed wire dominated the countryside, snaking its way up and down the roads, around the villages and through the fields. Guard towers rose high in the air, dwarfing all other structures. In each one, a soldier silently watched for Viet Cong, his M-16 rifle always at the ready."

After being introduced to the nurses already working at the 90th, she asked them if the area was safe, given that everything looked so battle-ready.

"Safe?" laughed one. "Honey, whoever fed you that line should be horsewhipped." She told Lynda that many nurses had already been wounded. She continued, "The V.C. don't care whether you're a nurse, a clerk, or an infantryman. All they know is that you're an American." And what made the situation particularly difficult, she said, was that the VC were essentially impossible to distinguish from the rest of the population.

Lynda's destination was the 71st Evacuation Hospital in Pleiku Province, near the Cambodian border, an area of heavy combat.

Lynda had heard that the casualties were "supposedly unending."

Her first shift shocked her: "There were *only* fifteen wounded soldiers who needed surgery. I saw young boys with their arms and legs blown off, some with their guts hanging out, and others with 'ordinary' gunshot wounds."

Lynda would remember her first few days in the operating room as "a blur of wounded soldiers, introductions to new colleagues and almost constant surgery during our twelve-hour shifts." And what surprised her most was that everyone kept saying this was a "slow period."

She began assisting a surgeon named Carl, who had a deserved reputation for saving lives in a near-miraculous manner. Carl could talk for hours on almost any topic and did so while performing surgeries. But when he became tired, the topic he returned to again and again was that his young patients were being shot to pieces for nothing.

Lynda begged to differ, telling him that "the war was a noble cause to preserve democracy," something she believed was certainly worth fighting and dying for.

"You really believe that?" Carl asked her quietly.

"Of course I do," she replied.

Lynda Van Devanter. *Buckley family and personal archives of Lynda Van Devanter*

"Is that why you always wear that rhinestone flag on the lapel of your fatigue shirt?"

"I think we should be proud of our country, Carl, and proud of our flag."

"So do I. But I'm afraid this time, we may find that our country is wrong," the surgeon said.

A week after arriving at the 71st Evacuation Hospital, Lynda attended a party at the Bastille—a large hooch that served as the hospital's social center. Less than an hour into the party, she heard an explosion. The room went black. Lynda dove into a corner, shaking with fear. A loudspeaker outside blared, "Attention all personnel. Take cover. Pleiku air base is under rocket attack. Security alert condition red."

Lynda was shocked to hear casual conversations: people discussing sports and patients. And as the flashes of the American return fire lit up the room, Lynda could see people dancing. She didn't understand why they weren't terrified.

When the siren stopped and everyone walked out of the party, she asked one of the medics, "How do you know it's over?"

"Don't worry," he replied. "Once it stops, that's it for the night. It never starts again. That's the way the V.C. work. It's all just harassment. They need target practice and we've got a nice red cross they can aim at."

Apparently the VC had also taken aim near Lynda's trailer. On her return from the party, she discovered an enormous crater only three feet away. The trailer's walls were covered with holes made by pieces of hot shrapnel. Inside, Lynda noticed with a chill that the explosion had caused an enormous light fixture to fall from the ceiling onto her own cot.

That night she experienced a mass-cal for the first time. Describing it later, she wrote:

The moans and screams of so many wounded were mixed up with the shouted orders of doctors and nurses. One soldier vomited on my fatigues while I was inserting an IV needle into his arm. Another grabbed my hand and refused to let go. A blond infantry lieutenant begged me to give him enough morphine to kill him so he wouldn't feel any more pain. A black sergeant went into a seizure and died while Carl and I were examining his small frag wound. "Duty, honor, country," Carl said sarcastically as he worked. "I'd like to have Richard Nixon here for one week."

Over the next three days, Lynda snatched bits of sleep whenever she could. She rarely knew if it was day or night. But when the mass-cal was over, Carl gave her the greatest compliment she could have wished for: "You're a good help, Lynda."

As they walked to the hooches, Lynda could hear the sound of guns and helicopters in the distance. She wondered how long it would be until the wounded of that battle would be brought to the 71st. The thought made her shudder.

Both too tired to sleep, Lynda and Carl talked for a long time, both "trying to sound philosophical about . . . death." Lynda finally broke down, crying and shaking. Carl tried to comfort her and wound up crying too.

"Why do they have to die, Carl?" Lynda asked.

"Who knows?" he replied.

"I don't understand," she said.

"Nobody does," he said.

But Lynda still felt proud of her country. Writing to her parents, she said:

At 4:16 a.m. our time the other day, two of our fellow Americans landed on the moon. At that precise moment,

Pleiku Air Force Base . . . sent up a whole skyful of flares—white, red, and green. It was as if they were daring the surrounding North Vietnamese Army to try and tackle such a great nation. As we watched it, we couldn't speak at all. The pride in our country filled us to the point that many had tears in their eyes.

It hurts so much sometimes to see the paper full of demonstrators, especially people burning the flag. Fight fire with fire, we ask here. Display the flag, Mom and Dad, please, everyday. And tell your friends to do the same. It means so much to us to know we're supported, to know not everyone feels we're making a mistake being here.

Every day we see more and more why we're here. When a whole Montagnard village comes in after being bombed and terrorized by Charlie, you know. There are helpless people dying everyday. The worst of it is the children. Little baby-sans being brutally maimed and killed. They've never hurt anyone.

One harmless civilian who lived in the area was Father Bergeron. He was a funny, kindhearted French priest who was full of stories and did all he could to ease the suffering around him. Because of his selflessness, the 71st staff bent the rules for him. For instance, they were only supposed to treat civilians with war-related wounds. But when Father Bergeron brought them civilians with diseases, such as a young girl with congestive heart failure, they couldn't refuse to help.

Father Bergeron hated the war. "Let the old glory mongers and politicians fight their own wars and let the young men and women get on with their lives," he would often say. He absolutely refused to take sides; his only aim was to help as many people as he could. Lynda assumed the VC loved him as much as

Lynda, February 1970.
*Buckley family and personal
archives of Lynda Van Devanter*

the staff at the 71st did.

It became brutally obvious one day that this was not the case. The 71st staff learned that the VC had tortured and killed Father Bergeron before displaying his remains in the middle of a village "as a warning to any American sympathizers."

That night Lynda was assisting a surgeon working to save the life of an enemy prisoner. When the surgeon spoke of getting even by doing to his patient exactly what the enemy had done to the beloved priest, Lynda knew he was just venting and would never actually do anything so barbaric. But something welling up inside her almost wished he would. In that dark moment, she felt she might have gladly assisted him.

Lynda had to work harder now to remind herself that she was "in Vietnam to save people who were threatened by tyranny." But she found that belief increasingly difficult to maintain as she "heard stories of corrupt South Vietnamese officials, US Army atrocities, and a population who wanted nothing more than to be left alone so they could return to farming their land."

In her letters home, she began to express her doubts about how the United States was handling the war: "It would be a lot easier if our government would just make up its mind. . . . We should either pull out of Vietnam or hit the hell out of the NVA. This business of pussyfooting around is doing nothing but harm. It's hurting our GIs, the people back home, and our image abroad."

Yet in the same letter, she admitted to being proud of her work: "I don't think there are many other places where you can feel as needed in nursing. . . . For the first time in my life, I feel like I have to keep going or people might not survive."

But the work was also taking its toll. "Holding the hand of one dying boy could age a person ten years," she wrote later. "Holding dozens of hands could thrust a person past senility in a matter of weeks."

Lynda discovered that she could no longer cry, which made her work somewhat easier. "If you can't feel, you can't be hurt," she wrote. "If you can't be hurt, you'll survive."

That all changed drastically a few months later when Lynda was in an officer's club with some friends watching a United Service Organizations (USO) show. While in the middle of her second drink, she imagined she saw the faces and bodies of the wounded, dying, and dead men she'd seen at the 71st, all of them appearing in heartbreaking detail in her mind.

"They were all with me in that room," she recalled later. "I tried to force them out of my mind. For a moment I did. Then all the images came crashing back on me."

She became hysterical and was escorted back to her hooch. A fellow nurse stayed with her all night, holding her, rocking her. Finally, around 5:00 in the morning, she fell asleep.

When she woke 24 hours later, Lynda felt numb. She threw away her rhinestone flag pin and went back to work.

In June 1970, when her yearlong tour was up, Lynda boarded a jet, her "freedom flight" out of Vietnam. "As the jet took off, I was filled with the most exhilarating sensation of my life . . . like the weight of a million years had been suddenly lifted from my shoulders," she said.

But when the bus from the airport dropped her and others off at the Oakland Army Terminal at 5:00 AM, they had no way of immediately reaching the San Francisco International airport, which was 20 miles away. Lynda decided to hitchhike her way there.

Dressed in her uniform, she watched car after car whiz by. Some of the drivers screamed obscenities at her. Others threw garbage. Finally, two friendly young men in a van stopped and offered her a ride. Relieved, Lynda tried to swing her duffle bag into the vehicle. Before she could do so, one of the men slammed the door shut.

"We're going past the airport, sucker, but we don't take Army pigs," he said. Then he spit on her, called her a Nazi, and drove away, the back wheels of the van showering her with dirt and stones.

"What had I done to him?" Lynda wondered. "Didn't they realize that those of us who had seen the war firsthand were probably more antiwar than they were? That we had seen friends suffer and die? That we had seen children destroyed? That we had seen futures crushed? Were they that naïve?"

Someone finally took pity on her, and eventually she made it back home to Virginia. On the first night she presented her family with a slide show of Vietnam photos. When she came to photos of the operating room, her uncomfortable parents asked if she could show them something "less gruesome." Lynda hid the slides away in the back of her closet. "I had learned quickly," she wrote later. "Vietnam would never be socially acceptable."

Years passed, and Lynda took a series of nursing jobs while suffering an intense emotional pain she couldn't shake or even begin to comprehend.

She eventually married a close friend who created a radio documentary called *Coming Home, Again*, relating Vietnam veterans' experiences. One of the men involved in her husband's project asked Lynda if she would agree to be interviewed for the documentary. Then he asked her to create the Vietnam Veterans of America (VVA) Women Veterans organization, to reach out to women veterans.

Lynda agreed. She also began studying post-traumatic stress disorder (PTSD) and realized it had been part of her life for years. She was certain that many other women veterans were also suffering from PTSD. Her Women Veterans project gave a voice to these women and helped them realize they were not alone.

She became the first American Vietnam military nurse to publish a widely read war memoir; her book, titled *Home Before Morning*, helped inspire the creation of *China Beach*, an award-winning TV series set in an American evacuation hospital during the Vietnam War.

The VVA honored her in 1982 with its Excellence in the Arts award and in 2002 with its Commendation Medal.

Lynda suffered from a vascular disease she believed was related to Agent Orange, a defoliant used by the US forces during the war.

She died at age 55 on November 15, 2002, and her death was widely mourned within the Vietnam veteran community. "Lynda's book stands as one of the most powerful, evocative, and influential Vietnam War memoirs," said Marc Leepson, the arts editor of the VVA's national newspaper, in an obituary for her. "*Home Before Morning* changed people's attitudes about the women who served in the Vietnam War, especially the nurses who faced the brutality of the war every day and whose service was all but ignored during the war and in the years immediately after."

AGENT ORANGE

Because Communist forces found cover under the lush vegetation growing in Vietnam during the war, the US military decided to destroy that cover by spraying it with powerful plant-killing defoliants—millions of gallons' worth. The most widely used of these was Agent Orange, so named because of the orange band around its storage barrels. Agent Orange was extremely successful in clearing ground cover, but it caused severe damage to everyone who came near it, both in the short and long term: Millions of Vietnamese and Americans who were exposed to Agent Orange later gave birth to or fathered children with severe disabilities. A similar number of veterans on both sides of the war developed fatal illnesses years later from their previous contact with the poisonous substance.

LEARN MORE

American Daughter Gone to War by Winnie Smith (Gallery Books, 1994).

Dreams That Blister Sleep: A Nurse in Vietnam by Sharon Grant Wildwind (River Books, 1999).

Home Before Morning: The Story of an Army Nurse in Vietnam by Lynda Van Devanter with Christopher Morgan (Beaufort Books, 1983).

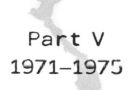

Part V
1971–1975

ENDINGS AND BEGINNINGS

★

IN FEBRUARY 1971, PRESIDENT Nixon's "Vietnamization" received a major test: Army of the Republic of Vietnam (ARVN) soldiers went up against North Vietnam Army (NVA) soldiers in what was called Operation Lam Son 719. The ARVN mission was to invade Laos in order to disrupt the flow of supplies down Ho Chi Minh Trail to the Vietnamese Communists in the South. It was a disastrous defeat for the ARVN troops, who were supplied with US airpower but no American ground forces.

But Nixon publicly claimed the operation a victory. Few Americans shared his opinion: polls taken regarding the president's handling of the war were sinking even lower than his general approval rating. A majority 58 percent of Americans now considered the war to be "morally wrong."

If Americans back home were growing disillusioned with the war, many US servicemen in Vietnam were even more so. Even apart from the deliberate My Lai slaughter, their military was responsible for a large and disheartening number of civilian casualties. And if President Nixon was really winding down America's involvement in the war and sending fighting men home, why were draftees still arriving? Search-and-destroy missions became "search-and-avoid" missions as draftees did whatever they could to survive their yearlong tours of duty. The use of marijuana, opium, and heroin, easily obtainable on the streets of Saigon, skyrocketed among a growing number of US servicemen, many of whom also created their own antiwar organizations and underground protest newspapers. Back home, Vietnam veterans were protesting the war as well: on April 22, 1971, more than 1,000 of them took their combat award medals and threw them onto the steps of the US Capitol.

While these events were enormously frustrating to Nixon, he remained determined to keep the United States in Vietnam until it was clear that the South could stand alone.

His anger reached new limits, however, when on June 13, 1971, the *New York Times* began publishing portions of the Pentagon Papers—7,000 pages of top-secret US documents and analyses regarding the Vietnam War. The documents proved that the previous administrations had been filled with individuals—including presidents—who had doubted the war's ultimate success from the very beginning. The United States had stayed in Vietnam not because its officials thought they could win the war but because they didn't want to be responsible for losing it.

The papers did not mention Nixon's administration—they stopped before his election—but the president was still furious, and he launched an unsuccessful attempt to shut down their publication.

Then, months later, while Secretary of State Henry Kissinger continued secret talks with leaders from both North and South Vietnam, Nixon put into action his own diplomacy plans:

on February 21, 1972, he stepped onto Chinese soil and met with Chairman Mao Zedong, initiating a thaw in relations between the two Cold War enemies that many hoped would reestablish diplomatic ties between their nations. America's staunch anti Communist president shaking hands with the second-most-powerful Communist leader in the world had seemed impossible only a short time before. The Hanoi government wished it was: if the United States and China normalized relations, as Nixon hoped, China might no longer support Hanoi's war.

The North Vietnamese government hardly needed a reason to undermine Richard Nixon. So, hoping to destroy his chances for reelection in November and testing the strength of South Vietnam with fewer Americans there, North Vietnamese forces launched the Eastertide Offensive, a major months-long attack in the South. As the Tet Offensive had virtually ended the possibility of Lyndon Johnson's reelection, so Hanoi officials hoped this Eastertide Offensive would do the same to Richard Nixon's reelection plans.

Instead Nixon responded with increased naval and air attacks on North Vietnamese infrastructure, military targets, and population centers. These continued throughout the summer of 1972 and always resulted in the outbreak of new American protests. These protests affected Nixon in an increasingly dangerous way: he began to view the demontrators as his personal enemies.

So while he waged an open war against the North, his administration waged a secret one against his fellow Americans. On June 17, 1972, five men were arrested for breaking into the offices of the Democratic National Headquarters, located in a Washington, DC, building called the Watergate. It was soon discovered that the men had been hired by the committee to reelect the president.

THE WATERGATE SCANDAL

On June 17, 1972, five men were arrested in the Watergate building complex in Washington, DC. They had been caught trying to plant listening devices in the headquarters of the Democratic National Committee, and it became immediately apparent that they had been hired by the committee to reelect President Nixon. The president publicly claimed he knew nothing of the specific incident (which is most likely true) until he'd read about it in the newspapers the following day. He promised a vigorous investigation. However, he and his aides immediately planned a cover-up: he ordered that the burglars be paid for their silence and used the FBI to lie about their motives. Why? President Nixon had secrets he feared might be uncovered by a lengthy investigation. From the beginning of his administration, he had been using the FBI and the CIA to spy on, harass, and destroy the reputations of approximately 200 people, most of them antiwar activists; one of the people targeted was Daniel Ellsberg, the man responsible for bringing the Pentagon Papers to light. When the president's illegal activities—along with his habit of taping every conversation that occurred inside the Oval Office—were revealed during the Watergate investigation, the House Judiciary Committee ordered the president to turn over his tapes. When he refused, the committee voted to impeach him for obstruction of justice. Nixon resigned on August 8, 1974, before Congress could vote on whether to bring formal articles of impeachment against him. The new president, Gerald R. Ford (Nixon's vice president), pardoned Nixon within a month, formally ending the investigation.

The Watergate scandal not only brought down the Nixon presidency but also was a major element in creating the bleak outlook many Americans had about their nation and government during the post–Vietnam War years.

But Nixon seemed unbeatable: neither the Eastertide Offensive nor the unfolding Watergate scandal prevented him from winning a landslide victory in the November 1972 presidential election.

Meanwhile, peace talks had stalled. South Vietnam's president Nguyen Van Thieu was unwilling to sign a peace agreement. Nixon tried to bring everyone back to the bargaining table in December by initiating an intense 11-day series of round-the-clock air attacks on Hanoi and Haiphong, another large North Vietnamese city. These so-called Christmas Bombings, officially named Operation Linebacker II, claimed the lives of more than 1,000 civilians and were condemned by many international figures.

Days after the bombings stopped, the peace talks resumed. And on January 27, 1973, representatives of the United States, North Vietnam, South Vietnam, and the Vietcong's new Provisional Revolutionary Government signed the Paris Peace Accords. Nixon had privately assured President Thieu that the United States would respond with military force should the North attack.

But he wouldn't be able to follow through on this promise: by the time the NVA had violated the Paris Peace Accord with an attack on the South on December, 13, 1974, Nixon was no longer president. Rather than face the impeachment charges voted on by the House Judiciary Committee, Nixon resigned, all the while claiming his innocence. The new president, Gerald R. Ford, could do nothing about the NVA violations of the Paris Accords: the year before, Congress had passed the Case-Church Amendment, which cut off US funds for any further military activity in Vietnam, Laos, or Cambodia.

President Ford gave a press conference in January 1975 and expressly stated that the United States would no longer assist

South Vietnam. The North wasted little time, and on April 30 NVA troops poured into Saigon as the last Americans were scrambling onto evacuation helicopters lifting off from the roof of the US embassy.

By 11:00 AM a Vietcong flag hung over a balcony of the presidential palace in Saigon. One young NVA soldier, entering the city for the first time, remarked to a local, "Why did you let us win? It will be terrible now."

He was right. The new Vietnamese government immediately sent hundreds of thousands of Vietnamese people with real or perceived ties to the Southern government or the United States to so-called reeducation centers where they lived in barracks and were forced to engage in manual labor and endure strident lectures on Communist ideology designed to purge their minds of Western ideas. Some remained imprisoned for years, while others died from the rough conditions, were executed, or took their own lives.

The United States and Communist Vietnam had an extremely difficult postwar relationship. President Ford, stating that the North Vietnamese had "repeatedly and in massive efforts violated the Paris Peace Accords" when they had invaded the South, refused to allow normal diplomatic or trade relations with the new Socialist Republic of Vietnam—a war-devastated nation desperately struggling to rebuild itself and survive on a rigid, government-controlled economy. "Yes, we defeated the United States," said Vietnamese prime minister Pham Van Dong. "But now we are plagued with problems. We do not have enough to eat. We are a poor, underdeveloped nation. Waging war is simple, but running a country is very difficult." Most Americans, deeply disillusioned with their government and each other, were in no mood for reconciliation with their former enemy either: approximately 58,000 young Americans had been killed in a war that had not resulted in victory. And 2,000 of these remained unaccounted for years after the war. This last issue remained the most serious and painful point of contention between the two nations for decades.

These problems, although difficult, were eventually worked out. And in 1997, 22 years after Graham Martin, the American ambassador to South Vietnam, had rushed into a helicopter from the roof of the US embassy in Saigon, the first postwar US ambassador to the Socialist Republic of Vietnam walked calmly through the doors of the brand-new US embassy in Hanoi.

But it was not the first time Colonel Douglas "Pete" Peterson had been there.

A veteran of the US Air Force, then Captain Peterson had been shot down over North Vietnam in 1966 and spent the next six and a half years in Hanoi's infamous Hoa Lo Prison. When diplomatic ties between Vietnam and the United States were fully restored in the 1990s, US president Bill Clinton asked him to be Vietnam's US ambassador.

Colonel Peterson had by then retired from the air force and also served three terms as a congressman. He wasn't initially interested in the president's offer but eventually decided to accept, having already put his pain in the past. "I didn't want to be measured on having been sitting in a cell for 6½ years," he said. "I wanted to be measured on what I could contribute into the future."

KATE WEBB

Captive Journalist

IN MARCH 1967, 23-YEAR-OLD New Zealand–born Kate Webb left her job in a Sydney, Australia, newsroom and headed for Vietnam. Why? "It was simply the biggest story going, and I didn't understand it," she wrote. Neither did Kate understand why, when Australia and New Zealand were sending their young men to fight in the war, their news agencies weren't also sending reporters there.

So she went, taking with her only a typewriter, the name of a United Press International (UPI) photographer, and a few hundred dollars.

Writing articles for Vietnamese newspapers for a few weeks brought in enough income to prevent Kate from starvation but not from becoming "seriously hungry." What's more, news agency editors constantly rebuffed her, sometimes, she guessed, because she looked much younger than she was. The time on her visa was running out, and she was no closer to understanding the war than she had been before leaving Australia.

Then Kate got a "stringing," or freelance, job with a GI newspaper. This gave her formal accreditation with the Military Assistance Command, Vietnam (MACV), an extended visa, the right to attend daily military briefings, and the right to accompany the fighting men into battle.

She was gaining an understanding of Saigon—its journalists, priests, bar girls, and street kids—but she wanted to learn more about the war itself. Months later, she did. The war—and the Vietnamese Communist fighters—came to that city in a big way. On January 30, 1968, Kate rushed to the besieged American embassy in Saigon to cover the Tet Offensive, becoming the first wire correspondent to do so. Her articles appeared in the *New York Times*, *Newsweek*, and *Time*. And Kate was glad to discover that she possessed a crucial trait for a war correspondent: she could "function and write amid the knife-edge fear of battle."

As Kate's options widened, she was free to pursue stories that interested her. She decided to spend time with Army of the Republic of Vietnam (ARVN) soldiers. She knew that American papers, intensely interested in their own "political clamor over the war," wouldn't likely be publishing her stories of these South Vietnamese soldiers. But she went with the soldiers anyway because they were one aspect of the war she didn't yet fully understand.

Kate knew that while the Americans could go home after their yearlong tours of duty, ARVN soldiers were required to remain in the war for its duration. For these men, the "dragging war usually spelled dishonor, death, injury, or imprisonment," she wrote. She followed them on their "pitch-black" night patrols, her way lit only by "the tiny phosphorous mark on the pack of the man in front" of her. They laughed at Kate's height—five feet seven inches—and her size-eight boots. But they also appreciated her because she did all she could to help

Kate in Vietnam. *Getty Images*

them: unlike the Americans, these men didn't have medical helicopter support. She helped them carry their wounded out of danger.

Kate's curiosity eventually led her to Cambodia. That nation was "engulfed in chaos and on the bum end of a war the United States was pulling out of with a final, wrenching kick," she wrote.

Nixon's attempt to bomb Vietnamese Communist sanctuaries across the Vietnam border in Cambodia had stirred up deep and desperate trouble within that country. On March 18, 1970, Cambodia's prime minister, Lon Nol, deposed Prince Norodom Sihanouk in a coup and established the Khmer Republic in Cambodia, which allied itself with the United States and sought to rid Cambodia of the Vietnamese Communists.

But Lon Nol had to fight another enemy, one emerging from his own nation: the Khmer Rouge, Cambodian Communists led by an intensely brutal leader named Pol Pot. The United States, in its quest to bomb the Vietnamese out of Cambodia, was also killing thousands of Cambodian civilians. Pol Pot used this destruction to stir up civilian hatred for the Americans—and for Lon Nol, a US ally. A civil war was born, and the Khmer Rouge—allied with the Vietnamese Communists—was on the rise.

The international press covered this civil war, regrouping every night in Cambodia's capital city of Phnom Penh. On the evening of October 28, 1970, Kate's UPI colleagues Frank Frosch—UPI's bureau chief in Cambodia—and Kyoichi Sawada—a Pulitzer Prize–winning photographer—didn't return. Their bodies were discovered the following day in a rice paddy next to a road referred to as Highway 2. Soldiers of the Khmer Rouge had executed the men; the Khmer Rouge never took prisoners. When a TV crew tried to film the bodies of the two men in the morgue, Kate lost control and tried to smash their cameras. When she was alone and calmer, she kept repeating one word to herself: "No."

This tragedy gave Kate a new job: Frank Frosch's. While Frank and Kyoichi had been alive, the three of them had spent many evenings in the UPI bungalow sitting below a huge map of Cambodia, discussing their day's work. Now Kate spent hours alone in the same spot staring at the map, as if doing so would help her make sense of the war.

Months later, on the night of April 6, 1971, Chea Ho, a Cambodian freelance reporter, joined her. He pointed to an area along Highway 4 where he said there would be fighting on the following day between Cambodian Lon Nol paratroopers and North Vietnamese Army (NVA) soldiers. He showed her how far the paratroopers hoped to go. He said he was going there to see for himself whether they would make it that far.

Was Kate interested? She told him she wasn't. But the following day, when she attended a military briefing and heard Chea Ho's story repeated, she knew she had to see how well the Lon Nol paratroopers would perform.

Taking with her a Cambodian translator named Chhim Sarath (whom she called Chhimmy), Kate drove to the rear lines of battle and continued to the front on foot. A half hour later, she and Chhimmy found themselves trapped when "fire burst from all sides." They huddled in a roadside ditch as bullets flew above them. As they crawled through the red dirt, they were eventually joined by four other trapped noncombatants: Tea Kim Heang, a Cambodian photographer; Eang Charoon, a Cambodian newspaper photographer and cartoonist; Toshiishi Suzuki, a Japanese journalist; and Vorn, Toshiishi's Cambodian interpreter.

The fight was over. The Cambodian soldiers were gone. The NVA soldiers remained. The civilians tried to quickly put as much distance as possible between themselves and the former battleground. They crawled for hours, suffering increasingly from thirst, insect bites, and scratches from the sharp elephant grass. Thirteen hours later, Kate wrote one last entry in the journal she kept: "April 8, 0200. This nightmare is stretching out too long. Gone past unbearable."

Later that morning, it would become much worse.

The civilians came face-to-face with two young men in NVA uniforms who motioned for the group to drop everything. Terrified, their hands in the air, the civilians all cried out, "Nha bao" (journalist), then "Nuoc" (water).

The soldiers stripped the civilians of their belongings, tied their hands behind them with baling wire that cut into their skin, linked them together into two groups of three, then moved them into a dark bunker. Kate assumed a live grenade would follow.

But she and the others were then brought back outside. It seemed the soldiers weren't sure what to do with them. A soldier handed Kate a small tin of water. Thinking they would all share it, she passed it around before taking a drink. It came back to her empty. "That the others hadn't left me anything, and what it meant, shocked me more than the rifles," she wrote later. "I said nothing, but there was a huge loneliness in my head that didn't leave me."

Still tied together, the group was forced to march. "I tasted it—the feeling of being a prisoner—underneath the burning thirst, the new loneliness in me," Kate wrote. And though she was certain they were going to be killed, she couldn't resist her reporter's "compulsive documenting of every detail" of her experience.

The soldiers hacked off tree branches, then placed them into the bound hands of the prisoners to keep them camouflaged from any passing planes.

Heading north, they "slipped like shadows through the villages and jungles, across paddy fields, and over mountains and small mountain streams, starting at dusk and stopping just before dawn."

After a blurred number of days and nights on foot, the prisoners and their captors stopped in a clearing. One by one, the soldiers singled out each prisoner for what they said were interviews. Thirty or forty minutes would pass, then a single shot would be heard. "As our numbers dwindled, we couldn't meet one another's eyes," Kate wrote later.

Her turn came. She was brought to a military man roughly in his 60s. Ever since her capture, Kate had been striving to view herself as more than a frightened prisoner and the group of them more than a herd of doomed cattle. Now, sitting before this military man, exhausted and ill though he appeared, Kate's hands shook with fear. She forced herself to remember that she was a respected journalist and the representative of an international news service.

"Do not be afraid," said the expressionless interpreter. "You are in the hands of the Liberation Armed Forces [the army of the Southern Vietnamese Communists]." The interpreter told Kate to speak slowly so that he could understand her English. He asked her for her name, rank, and nationality. She gave her name and nationality but no rank, insisting that she wasn't part of the military. She measured each word with great care.

The questions droned on and on. The interviewer asked about her family, what each member did for a living, and how much each was paid. Finally, he came to the point.

"Why were you down on Highway 4?"

"To find out what was happening," Kate replied.

"Why would you risk your life to find out what was happening?"

"Now I wish I hadn't but I am a reporter."

"Why were you with the Lon Nol Troops?"

"I wasn't with them," Kate answered, explaining that she had followed them in her own car.

He asked what she thought of the war. Kate said it was "too long." He asked why it was so long, and Kate responded that the different groups of people could not agree on what was most important.

"An odd thing happened as question followed question and the young interpreter struggled to translate from English," she wrote later. "I found myself thinking of the senior officer interrogating me as a professional soldier. The flip side of that was that I stopped feeling like a filthy, scared prisoner from the other side . . . probably on my way to execution, and like a professional reporter instead. He was taking what the war dealt out to him, and I was taking what the war dealt out to me."

When the interview was over, Kate was led down a narrow path. To her surprise, it led to a clearing where she found the rest of the prisoners, all of them very much alive.

The marching resumed until they stopped at a shelter near a military complex days later. The soldiers interrogated the prisoners again and gave what Kate described as "history lessons": the war from the Communist point of view.

By this time, the prisoners' health was in a precarious state. Everyone had lost too much weight. And Kate was experiencing severe symptoms: vomiting, diarrhea, fever, and shivering.

But what disturbed her more than her deteriorating physical condition was what was happening to her mind and emotions. Living inside "the gray limbo of the prisoner . . . with no links to the living world" made her fear she was descending into a dark place.

Three simple events had a surprisingly positive effect on Kate's dangerous psychological state. One day she abruptly decided to stand on her head. This simple act—along with the astonished reaction of everyone around her—raised her spirits profoundly.

The second event occurred after her return from a daylong interrogation. Toshiishi sat Kate down under a tree and led her through the steps of a Japanese tea ceremony using an empty condensed milk can.

Then one morning Kate was struck by the profound but simple beauty of "dawn reflected upside down in a dewdrop hanging from a leaf."

Finally, following a "tense new round of interrogations" at the same location, the soldiers told the prisoners they were being released. Kate didn't allow herself to believe it. "Hope, we had fast learned, was as treacherous as an oasis mirage, and as cruel," she said.

The prisoners were taken to the command hut. Every soldier and officer seemed to be there. The prisoners sat down on wooden benches in a semicircle around a table. An officer stood behind the table and began to read from a piece of paper, an official document that had apparently been translated into English. Kate was so ill at this point she had trouble concentrating on his exact words, but the officer appeared to be announcing their release. When he was finished, the prisoners were given a signal to clap. They clapped. They were each directed to sign the statement before their belongings were returned to them, minus notes and photographs. These, they were told, had been "liberated."

Then began what Kate called the "Mad Hatter's tea party." Tea was served, along with bananas, candy, and cigarettes. The hungry guards, Kate recalled, "hogged into the candy with more gusto" than the prisoners did. The captors asked the prisoners if they wanted to make thank-you statements into a tape recorder for their "humane treatment." As they hadn't been actually tortured, four of the prisoners, including Kate, agreed.

Then they were off with six guards. On the way, one of the guards repeatedly discussed the release plans with Toshiishi and Kate. It was a dangerous situation for all of them, the guards included, because they would be walking out of NVA and Vietcong-controlled territory. Kate wondered why these Communists were risking the lives of six of their men in order to release the captives.

After two days, she woke in the middle of the night to see everyone scrambling to gather their things. Then, amid hasty good-bye handshakes, the guards left their prisoners, who now "stood alone in the dark on a roadside in no-man's land." Terrified without their guards, the former prisoners eventually walked toward a group of Lon Nol soldiers and officers. Kate—in front of the group so they would seem less threatening—waved a white piece of parachute material the Vietnamese captors had given her, and they all yelled, *"Kassat, kassat"* (press, press).

They had been in captivity for 23 days.

"Miss Webb," cried one officer, recognizing Kate, "you're supposed to be dead!" Kate had been assumed dead because everyone thought the Khmer Rouge had captured her and someone had discovered the body of a woman resembling her.

As she recovered from two types of malaria, Kate's transition from captivity to freedom was perhaps the strangest and in some ways the most difficult aspect of her experience. Aside from receiving a "bizarre mixture of fan and hate mail," she realized that her communication skills had fundamentally altered. Although she was free, she found herself choosing each word with the utmost care, as if her survival, and that of those around her, still depended on it.

Something else she found quite disturbing was the deeply divided US press. She was shocked when, speaking to the members of the Washington Press Club, she was told that "a field reporter was morally bound to take a hawk [prowar] or dove [propeace] stand."

Kate argued that the field reporter's job was not to choose sides but only to report "what was happening and what people were saying, feeling, and doing on the ground. Without that hard, unbiased input," she said, there was "nothing to opinionate, or stand, on."

When the Vietnam War ended, Kate noted that many of its reporters had trouble coping with peacetime: "There were suicides and divorces, a lot of editors saying what do we do with these madmen, and quite a few of us madmen not knowing what to do with ourselves."

But she continued to work as a journalist, often facing dangerous situations to do so. While covering the Soviet occupation of Afghanistan, she was nearly scalped when a militiaman dragged her up a flight of stairs by her hair. And while covering the assassination of India's former prime minister Rajiv Gandhi, she almost lost an arm during a motorcycle accident.

Kate died from cancer in Sydney, Australia, on May 13, 2007, at age 64. Her *New York Times* obituary quoted a fellow Vietnam reporter, Pulitzer Prize–winning Peter Arnette, who said that Kate was a "fearless action reporter" and "one of the earliest— and best—women correspondents of the Vietnam War."

LEARN MORE

"Highpockets" by Kate Webb, in *War Torn: Stories of War from the Women Reporters Who Covered Vietnam* by Tad Bartimus et al. (Random House, 2002).

On the Other Side: 23 Days with the Vietcong by Kate Webb (Quadrangle Books, 1972).

JOAN BAEZ

Protest Singer

JOAN BAEZ WAS AT THE White House. A rising star of the folk music movement, she had been invited to perform there, with several other entertainers, in a gala for President John F. Kennedy. But the president had been shot before the performance date. Shortly after his shocking assassination in November 1963, Joan received a message from the staff of the new president, former vice president Lyndon B. Johnson, assuring her that the gala would go on as planned.

She went, dedicating one of her songs to Jacqueline Kennedy, the former First Lady. Then, before singing "The Times They Are a-Changin'," a new Bob Dylan song, she pleaded with President Johnson to keep Americans out of Vietnam.

Joan already knew how to use her beautiful singing voice to promote causes she believed in. Earlier that year, on August 28, 1963, she had sung "We Shall Overcome," the civil rights movement anthem, in DC at the March on Washington for Jobs and

Freedom before her good friend Martin Luther King Jr. gave his famous "I Have a Dream" speech.

After Joan's successful appearance at the presidential gala, a representative from Young Democrats for Johnson asked her to be one of their spokespeople. President Johnson was eager to win the 1964 election, to prove he could become president in his own right. He wanted Joan's help.

She responded to President Johnson directly, writing him that she would consider the offer only if he would "quit meddling around in Southeast Asia." The Young Democrats for Johnson didn't call again.

Joan would indeed have a powerful influence on young men and women, but not in the way President Johnson had hoped. Although he wanted his legacy to be the Great Society—a series

Joan at the March on Washington for Jobs and Freedom in 1963.
Wikimedia Commons

of laws attempting to eliminate poverty and racial injustice in the United States—he would instead be remembered as the American president most responsible for escalating US involvement in the Vietnam War. And Joan would be remembered for being one of that war's most prominent opponents.

After Johnson won the 1964 election, Joan had "a quiet revelation." Realizing that the US involvement in Vietnam was going to end up a "disaster," she decided to make a symbolic gesture of protest. Since approximately 60 percent of the national budget at that time went to the military, Joan refused to pay 60 percent of her federal income taxes. She wrote a lengthy letter to the IRS—and released it to the press—informing them of her plan and explaining in great detail why she could not support the manufacture of weapons of war. Not only did the weapons destroy lives, she wrote, but also the United States was spending far too much of its budget on the war. Newspapers across the country published the letter.

When an IRS official threatened Joan with jail time for tax evasion, she shrugged, saying, "Well, I imagine I'll go to jail sometime. It might as well be over something I really believe in."

"But jail's for bad people!" the IRS official cried.

"You mean like Jesus?" replied Joan, smiling. "And Gandhi?"

Joan *would* go to jail—twice in 1967 for protesting the war directly outside of the Oakland, California, military draft induction center—but never for income tax evasion, although she continued to pay only 40 percent of her federal income tax for the next 10 years. The IRS decided to get the other 60 percent by sending their agents to her concerts to take money from the concert register. Joan didn't mind. At least she wasn't giving it to them willingly: they had to spend their own time and effort to get it.

Her growing notoriety resulted in frequent invitations to appear on TV talk shows. The hosts would often invite her to appear along with someone who was anti-Communist and enthusiastic about America's involvement in Vietnam. Joan would take these opportunities to appeal directly to the

PROTEST SONGS OF THE VIETNAM WAR

Prior to 1967, prowar songs such as "Hello Vietnam," "Dear Uncle Sam," and "The Ballad of the Green Berets" actually outnumbered antiwar songs broadcast on American radio. Popular songs such as "Blowin' in the Wind," "Where Have All the Flowers Gone," "Eve of Destruction," and "Masters of War" (the last two written in the early 1960s to protest the Cold War's nuclear arms buildup) became widely used by antiwar protestors later in the decade. As the war progressed and the protest movement gained momentum, some artists wrote and released songs—such as "I Ain't Marching Anymore" and "Universal Soldier"—that could be heard more often at protest rallies and coffeehouses than on the radio because some stations banned them.

Though it was not written as a protest song, "We Gotta Get Out of This Place" eventually became an anthem of the American fighting men in Vietnam, who frequently requested it of the bands hired to entertain them. They also loved the protest song "Fortunate Son," a complaint about how wealthy young men could often avoid being sent to Vietnam.

"Give Peace a Chance," arguably the most famous protest song of the war, was both played on the radio and sung at protest rallies: in November 1969, it was sung by hundreds of thousands of people who had gathered for an antiwar protest in Washington, DC.

mothers in the live studio audience. She'd ask them about the busses arriving at the induction centers each morning. Were they "filled with young men ready to give their lives for their country," she asked, or were those new draftees merely "young boys who were terrified and were there only because they'd gotten a letter in the mail telling them they had no choice"?

But Joan wanted to do more. And she wanted to learn more. While her instincts had led her to become a major voice in the antiwar movement, she wanted to gain a more solid academic and historical foundation of the concepts of peaceful protest. So in 1965 she and her friend and mentor Ira Sandperl began an organization called the Institute for the Study of Nonviolence. Joan purchased a building in Carmel Valley, California, and charged attending students nominal fees, provided them with reading lists, encouraged them to meditate and engage in discussions, and invited them to attend lectures and seminars from peace activists and speakers from all over the world.

The institute also helped young men in need of moral support if they chose to oppose their own military drafts. One young man named Billy, who had been corresponding with Joan for four months, had finally decided to go AWOL (absent without leave) from the army. He visited Joan before he turned himself in to the military authorities.

He told her that during his training he and other draftees had been brought into a chapel and told that, although one of the Bible's 10 Commandments was "Do not kill," the military was going to teach them how to do just that. The trainer asked the young men if that was right. Before they could answer the question, he did: "Yes, it's right to kill because you're killing for your country!"

Billy had prepared a statement to hand to the military authorities, part of which read, "I will not bring myself to bear down and fire with intent to kill another human being. I do not call myself a good, pure Christian person, my life has shown that I am not. But I found peace in myself with God in denying to kill."

After working nearly full-time at the institute for a few years, Joan opened a branch of Amnesty International—a human rights organization—on the West Coast before she resumed a hectic schedule of concerts.

She was on the road in December 1972 when she received an opportunity to take a closer look at the war she had been protesting for so long. Cora Weiss, a leader of the Women Strike for Peace (WSP)—an organization begun in 1961 to protest nuclear testing and later also to try to end US involvement in Vietnam—said WSP was organizing trips for Americans to Hanoi, the capital of North Vietnam, in an attempt to create friendly relationships between American and North Vietnamese civilians. Would Joan like to go?

Joan agreed and was soon on a plane with three American men: lawyer and ex–brigadier general Telford Taylor; Episcopalian minister Rev. Michael Allen; and Barry Romo, a Vietnam veteran who was now against the war.

Their tour was carefully designed to show these four Americans the damage their military had inflicted on the people of North Vietnam. On the first day, Joan took an opportunity to speak to her tour guide about the ideals of nonviolence, saying that the Vietminh resistance had at one point been a peaceful movement. The guide laughed. Nonviolence was not appropriate in this war, he said.

On the first evening after dinner, the Americans were treated to some Vietnamese songs. Joan sang as well, dedicating her performance of "Sam Stone"—a song about a drug-addicted veteran—to all the people from both sides who had died in the

war. Barry wept through her entire performance. The Vietnamese people at the dinner surrounded him in a protective way, as
if, Joan thought, they were trying to shield him from further
pain and let him know that they had forgiven him for his part
in the war.

During the next two days, the North Vietnamese showed
their American visitors propaganda films and photos of dead
civilians and gave long lectures on what specific areas the
American military had bombed. Since Joan had long been protesting the war, she was annoyed with these enforced activities
and longed to explore Hanoi on her own.

On the third evening, December 18, she was feeling sick
from watching yet another graphic propaganda film and was
about to retire to her room for the night when the electricity
in the building failed. Two long, loud sirens rang out. One of
the Vietnamese men excused himself calmly, saying it was an
"alert."

All the hotel guests walked toward a nearby bomb shelter.
Because everyone seemed so relaxed, Joan thought she must
be the only nervous one in the group. Then she heard the roar
of planes. Everyone jumped and ran down the narrow flight of
stairs. An explosion shook the walls.

When the bombing stopped, someone joked that, because it
was December, perhaps the raid was an early Christmas present to Hanoi from President Nixon. Everyone laughed. But this
series of raids—technically referred to as Operation Linebacker
II and specifically designed to intimidate the North into recom-
mencing peace talks—would actually become known as the
Christmas Bombings.

Ten more bombing raids occurred that night. In the morning, the Americans walked through a demolished village on the
outskirts of Hanoi. Large craters were everywhere. Joan saw

Left to right: Rev. Michael Allen, Joan Baez, and Barry Romo walking through Hanoi's international airport after American B-52 airplanes had bombed it. *Getty Images*

people hunting through the wreckage, apparently looking for lost items. One girl bitterly asked Joan and the other Americans if they were there to "look at Nixon's peace."

Ten tense nights of bombing followed (with the exception of Christmas Day), and each morning, the Americans were invited to view the damage created the night before. When Joan saw a bombed hospital and a dead elderly woman laid out on the street, she broke down and sobbed uncontrollably.

During one raid, sophisticated Soviet antiaircraft guns and missiles shot down six American flyers. Bandaged and in shock, the American prisoners were forced to participate in a press conference. They each identified themselves and were allowed to give a message to the American press. One called the war "terrible" and said he hoped it would "end real soon." Considering the damage the raids had caused, Joan thought the North Vietnamese conducted the press conference with amazing self control.

But on the following night, she discovered that this restraint had a cruel edge. The Vietnamese were treating the prisoners inhumanely, including not allowing them into a shelter during the next raid. Instead the prisoners remained in their shoddy prison bunkhouses, which US bombs had already partially destroyed. Joan and the other Americans went to visit them. The prisoners seemed frightened and confused. One of them showed Joan a large piece of shrapnel that had come through the barracks ceiling. He asked her what was happening.

Joan, surprised by the question, explained with a bit of sarcasm how the American bombings were causing this type of damage.

"What I mean is, Kissinger said peace was at hand, isn't that what he said?" the POW asked.

Joan's sarcasm disappeared. She wanted to cry.

"That's what he said," she replied. "Maybe he didn't mean it."

Then she asked them if they'd like her to sing. They requested "The Night They Drove Old Dixie Down," Joan's most recent hit, a song about the Civil War from the Confederate perspective. She sang it. Then they all sang "Kumbaya" before Joan embraced each prisoner and left for the safety of the bomb shelter.

One morning after a particularly damaging bombing raid, the Vietnamese took Joan to a devastated area. There a woman stood where her home had once been. She was crying, repeating the same phrase over and over. Joan asked for an interpreter. The woman was crying, "My son, my son. Where are you now, my son?"

When Joan returned to the United States, she distilled 15 hours of recordings she had made during her trip—Vietnamese warning sirens, American bombing raids, her own singing in the bomb shelter, and the laughter of Vietnamese children—into a new album. She dedicated her unusual new record to the Vietnamese people and called it *Where Are You Now, My Son?*

In 1979, five years after the United States had withdrawn from Vietnam, Joan spoke out publicly against the new Socialist Republic of Vietnam. In a letter published in four major US newspapers, she criticized the brutal reeducation centers that were forcing a Communist worldview upon the people of South Vietnam. She wrote, "Instead of bringing hope and reconciliation to war-torn Vietnam, your government has created a painful nightmare." She maintained that her new protest was perfectly consistent with her previous antiwar stance, saying, "My politics have not changed. I have always spoken for the oppressed people of Vietnam who could not speak for themselves."

Throughout the years and to this day, Joan has continued to lend her support for causes she believes in strongly, always accompanied by her singing and always in a manner that promotes the fundamentals of nonviolence. In August 2009 she again affirmed her commitment to peace. Before giving a concert in Idaho Falls, Idaho, she was told there were four Vietnam veterans outside protesting her appearance.

She immediately went outside to meet them. One was holding a sign that read, JOAN BAEZ GAVE COMFORT & AID TO OUR ENEMY IN VIETNAM & ENCOURAGED THEM TO KILL AMERICANS!

The veterans told her that decades earlier they had felt betrayed and hurt by American antiwar protestors who had lashed out at the servicemen upon their return from Vietnam. Joan listened to them quietly and then explained that she had never engaged in that sort of abuse, that she had always supported Vietnam veterans.

Her sincere friendliness diffused their anger, and before long, they asked her to sign their posters. She agreed to sign the backs, not the fronts, where the denigrating words were printed.

Later, during the concert, Joan dedicated a song to the veterans she had just met. "You know, they just wanted to be heard," she explained. "Everyone wants to be heard. I feel like I made four new friends tonight."

LEARN MORE

And a Voice to Sing With: A Memoir by Joan Baez (Summit Books, 1987).

Daybreak by Joan Baez (Dial, 1966).

Where Are You Now, My Son? by Joan Baez (Pickwick Records, 1973).
Joan's vinyl album of poetry and singing against a backdrop of sounds recorded in Hanoi during the 1972 Christmas Bombings.

TRACY WOOD

"They're the Story"

ON MARCH 30, 1972, Bill Landry, foreign editor for United Press International (UPI), told reporter Tracy Wood she was next in line to go to Vietnam.

Up until that moment, Tracy's plans had not included that war-torn country. She was working at UPI's cable desk in New York City while learning Chinese. Nixon had visited China the previous month, and Tracy had been promised a spot on UPI's first China-bound news team when the Communist nation opened its borders to Western journalists.

And the Vietnam War, which was winding down, had already been part of Tracy's life for years: one New Jersey neighbor from her youth had been killed in Vietnam, and a high school friend was currently serving there as a helicopter medevac pilot. Tracy had also covered US war demonstrations before transferring to New York and, for the past seven months, had edited many reports coming out of Saigon.

But as soon as Bill invited her, she changed her plans.

"When do I leave?" she asked him.

Bill paused. Then he told Tracy that while his superiors wanted her to go, he did not. "I don't believe women should cover wars," he said.

Tracy was speechless. "For the first time in my life, someone in a position to decide my future was telling me that because I was a woman, I wasn't good enough," she wrote later.

Bill broke the silence and clarified his reasoning. "If anything happened to you," he said, "I'd feel bad."

"Landry had just articulated the problem that for generations held women back," Tracy wrote later. "Not conviction that women couldn't do the job. Something much harder to fight: well-meaning men in positions of authority who honestly believed it was more important to protect women from risks than encourage them to reach for the stars."

She said nothing aloud and instead made plans to go over Bill's head. He might be her immediate supervisor, but if those above him wanted her to go to Vietnam, she was going.

When her plans were set, she chose her arrival wardrobe carefully. She wanted to exude professionalism during her first meeting with her new boss, Saigon bureau chief Arthur Higbee, a journalist with three decades of impressive international work.

But her choice of a skirt, panty hose, and heels turned out to be a dreadful mistake. A few days after her arrival in Vietnam, Arthur told her to stay away from combat. "You're too feminine," he said. Before coming to Saigon, Tracy hadn't realized that even in the Southern city's relative safety, female reporters dressed like men: jeans and T-shirts or combat fatigues. "Don't become like the others," Arthur urged her. "Stay feminine."

She could cover stories about politics, refugees, hospitals, and diplomatic receptions, he said, but not the war itself. "I couldn't let this happen," Tracy wrote later. "I was a full reporter, not a partial reporter." But because Arthur was her top authority—she couldn't go over his head—Tracy would have to find her own way into combat reporting.

Her first attempt was a helicopter tour an American province adviser arranged. It wasn't exactly combat, but Tracy would be able to observe, from a distance, an area the North Vietnamese Army (NVA) had recently overrun and that the Army of the Republic of Vietnam (ARVN), supported by US Marines, was fighting to take back.

"You don't want anything to obstruct their field of fire," the adviser said to her. He was pointing to two ARVN soldiers—door gunners—guarding the two doorless entryways on opposite sides of the helicopter. When the helicopter took off, these soldiers sat down on the helicopter's floor, facing out, their legs dangling in the air.

The two US pilots flew past beautiful beaches that they said were hiding deadly mines. They demonstrated various helicopter flying techniques, one of them "a hard sideways turn" during which Tracy was "staring straight down at the earth through the missing doors." They skimmed the treetops. "Heading dead straight for a line of tall trees," she wrote later, "the pilots pulled up just in time to keep the skids from pruning the upper branches."

"Cowboys," shouted the smiling US adviser, trying to be heard over the engine. "Good practice. When they fly like this in combat, the North Vietnamese don't see them until it's too late."

Tracy attempted to calmly respond to his comment when the door gunners began firing their M60s at the ground. The helicopter twisted sharply and turned. This was no stunt. Tracy grabbed hold of the seat with both hands. Her camera and tape recorder swung in all directions from her neck.

Tracy Wood. *Ed Bassett*

The helicopter had strayed into NVA-controlled territory.

Once they were safely back on the ground, the adviser reassured Tracy that it wasn't easy to shoot down a helicopter from the ground. It had to be hit in a particular way. But they had definitely been hit. He showed her the bullet holes near the helicopter's tail and near the front. Then he pointed out one that had gone through an empty seat directly behind Tracy's.

"Well, we can't tell Arthur," said fellow UPI reporter Barney Seibert when Tracy related her day's events. "He'll have a fit you didn't follow his orders." Barney had covered the Korean War and had been in Vietnam for more than a year. He told Tracy, in secret, everything she wanted to know about combat reporting. He showed her how to use a handgun—some combat journalists carried them, he said, while others did not—and advised her to drive right through potholes in Vietcong-controlled territory. Knowing how well Americans cared for their cars, the Vietcong always mined the areas beside potholes.

But the most important piece of advice Barney gave her was to remember her role: "We're only reporters. What happens to us, what we think, what we feel, what we experience, doesn't matter. We're here to cover the war. Anytime we get too scared, too sick of it, too tired, we can hop on a plane and go home. The military and civilians can't do that. They're stuck. *They're* the story, not us."

A short time later, Tracy was accompanying an ARVN unit that worked with a US Army major. He complained to her about the hopeless corruption of the South Vietnamese army. She would come to understand this more thoroughly as time went on, writing later:

> Bribery was so commonplace at all levels of the Vietnamese government that it took routine under-the-table cash payments to get ordinary shipments through airport customs. And it ran so deep that cash could buy a man's way out of the South Vietnamese military or get him promoted, regardless of qualifications. Corruption badly weakened the South Vietnamese military. Men in the bottom ranks fought and died but often were led by patronage appointees at the top who frequently disappeared when things got tough.

The highway they were on had a dirt embankment on one side that led down from the road to open rice fields. Tracy saw a puff of dirt from the embankment fly straight up into the air. Then another, this one just behind their jeep. "I lost all sensation, including fear. . . . I felt nothing, not even the jarring crash of the jeep's wheels slamming through potholes. I heard no sounds, not the rush of wind through the open jeep, not the racket of combat, not the shouts of my compatriots. Only curiosity remained. My eyes took in every detail of those mesmerizing puffs of dirt," she wrote later.

They were driving through what was referred to as a "contested zone"—an area that kept switching from ARVN to NVA control—and a section of road where many reporters had already been shot at. The major pressed his boot down on the jeep's accelerator. It was impossible to turn off the road. There was one choice and one direction: keep moving, straight ahead. Tracy looked to her right. NVA soldiers were firing at the speeding jeep with their AK-47 rifles.

The ARVN soldiers in the back of the jeep returned fire with their M16s. Tracy was suddenly aware of "a massive hammering" in her head. Her steel helmet was pulled down as far as possible over her head while she hunched her shoulders so that the sleeveless bulletproof flak jacket would also cover her neck. But her arms and lower body were unprotected. She had to think, but she couldn't because of the pounding in her head.

She turned toward the major. "His left hand was on the steering wheel. His mouth was wide open in a shout lost to the racket of war," Tracy wrote later. "One word seemed to come faintly through the clamor. Down! I read it on his lips more than heard his voice. Down!"

She finally understood what was causing the pain in her head. The major had been pounding on her steel helmet. She immediately curled up into a ball and squeezed herself into the tiny area between the jeep's seat and dashboard until they were out of danger.

Tracy had been in Vietnam nearly a year when on January 23, 1973, US president Richard Nixon made his "Peace with

EXCERPTS FROM PRESIDENT NIXON'S "PEACE WITH HONOR" SPEECH:

A cease-fire, internationally supervised, will begin at 7 p.m., this Saturday, January 27, Washington time. Within 60 days from this Saturday, all Americans held prisoners of war throughout Indochina will be released. There will be the fullest possible accounting for all of those who are missing in action. During the same 60-day period, all American forces will be withdrawn from South Vietnam. . . .

In particular, I would like to say a word to some of the bravest people I have ever met—the wives, the children, the families of our prisoners of war and the missing in action. . . . Nothing means more to me at this moment than the fact that your long vigil is coming to an end.

Honor" speech. All remaining US forces would withdraw from Vietnam, and North Vietnam would release in stages all American POWs it was currently holding.

On February 12, 1973, the first group of POWs was released from Hanoi's infamous Hoa Lo Prison. Tracy was determined to witness the release of subsequent prisoners. But so was every other reporter in Saigon, as well as top international correspondents. Tracy would need inside help. She tried one of Nixon's old friends whom she knew from a previous UPI assignment. He said Nixon didn't want reporters and photographers present during the release.

She would have to work with someone in the North Vietnamese government. Delegates from the North were currently being housed in Saigon for the peace process and were only allowed outside for official meetings. As part of her job, Tracy talked by phone to them almost every night, and in most conversations, she managed to mention that she would love to cover the upcoming release of the American POWs.

It worked, and on March 15, Tracy was one of three reporters—she the only American—waiting outside of the Hoa Lo Prison, or the Hanoi Hilton, as the brutalized American POWs referred to it.

Some of the prisoners were standing at the iron-barred windows of their cells, while others were outside. Tracy couldn't yet see their faces, but "something in their posture made me uneasy," she wrote. "They were only a day away from freedom, and I'd expected them to be energized." They weren't. Both the POWs and the reporters had been forbidden to communicate before the release was final. When Tracy and the other two reporters tried to whisper to the prisoners, they received no response. There had been rumors of torture, of forced statements, but the journalists didn't know the details. As she watched the prisoners, she was "nagged by something terribly wrong."

Suddenly, she understood what it was, writing later:

They had no identity.

Even from a reasonable distance, I can identify friends, including those in the military, by the way they walk and hold their shoulders, their general posture.

These men had no posture.

Or they all had the same posture.

They were unidentifiable, taller and shorter, darker and lighter versions of the same man. Their faces had the same lack of expression; they walked the same, stood the same. No one stuck out in the crowd.

Only long practice could have caused that total loss of individuality—practice and a deathly need to be obscure. . . . This was primitive survival.

Tracy also managed to be present three weeks later when the last American POWs were released from Hoa Lo. The two dozen men seemed nervous, unsure about whether or not they were allowed to acknowledge the many US reporters, photographers, and television crews who had arrived to record the event.

Reporters at the release of the last American POWs from Hoa Lo Prison. Left to right: Keyes Beech, *Chicago Daily News*; Walter Cronkite, CBS; Tracy Wood, United Press International; Hugh Mulligan, Associated Press. *Tracy Wood*

A familiar face passed by the window outside.

"Is that *really* Walter Cronkite?" asked a young prisoner. The beloved and respected newsman known as "the Most Trusted Man in America" had just walked by. As always, Cronkite was quiet, professional, and polite as he talked with the POWs.

After the war, Tracy worked as an investigative reporter for the *Los Angeles Times* before becoming the investigations editor for the *Orange County Register*. Currently, she is senior writer at the online California news organization Voice of Orange County.

Tracy has won numerous awards for investigative reporting and in 2001 was named Los Angeles Print Journalist of the Year by Sigma Delta Chi, a professional journalism association.

In 2002 she and eight other female Vietnam War reporters coauthored a book, *War Torn*, detailing their wartime experiences.

LEARN MORE

Defiant: The POWs Who Endured Vietnam's Most Infamous Prison, the Women Who Fought for Them, and the One Who Never Returned by Alvin Townley (Thomas Dunne Books, 2014).

"Spies, Lovers, and Prisoners of War" by Tracy Wood, in *War Torn: Stories of War from the Women Reporters Who Covered Vietnam* by Tad Bartimus et al. (Random House, 2002).

"A War Correspondent Turned Lifelong Corruption Fighter" by Tracy Wood, Voice of Orange County, April 29, 2015, http://voiceofoc.org/2015/04/a-war-correspondent-turned-lifelong-corruption-fighter/.

KIM PHUC

Running from War

IN THE SOUTHERN VIETNAMESE city of Tien Gang one day in late April 1981, an 18-year-old woman was summoned from her premedical studies classroom. Four men were in the hallway asking for her.

When she came into the hallway, the men just stared at her.

"You are Kim Phuc?" one of them finally asked.

"Yes—I am Kim Phuc," the girl answered.

"*You* are the girl in the picture?" the man asked.

"Yes," she replied. "I am the girl in the picture."

This woman looked far too normal, too healthy to be the one they sought. The famous photo they spoke of had been taken nine years earlier, on June 8, 1972, during an event that nearly ended the girl's life.

A few days before the photo was taken, Kim's family had fled their home because the Vietcong (VC) was pressuring the Phucs to work for them. The Phucs found refuge in a temple with other South Vietnamese families and some soldiers of the Army of the

Republic of Vietnam (ARVN). Though the sounds of battle were far away, the soldiers warned that a "big attack" was coming.

Then the distinct smell of explosives became stronger. The sounds of war—planes, helicopters, bursting shells, and machine gun fire—grew louder.

The villagers heard the soldiers cursing: they had just seen one of their own observation planes trail the colored smoke used to identify the presence of VC. Had the pilot seen the enemy in this area? Or had he just made a terrible error?

"Everybody get out!" the soldiers shouted. "They are going to destroy everything!" The soldiers ran in the direction of the American base, urging the villagers on: "Run! Run fast, or you will die!"

Vietnamese photographer Nick Ut, along with a dozen other international journalists, was nearby waiting behind some ARVN barbed wire. They had heard rumors of an impending battle. Nick watched an ARVN Skyraider plane approach. He took a few photos.

Thinking that nothing else notable would occur that day, Nick was about to leave when he noticed something terribly wrong: the Skyraider pilot seemed to be off course. Then he saw a second Skyraider approach, this one "even more off target than the first."

Although they could tell something was dangerously off-kilter, the journalists knew better than to run away: American or ARVN soldiers might assume anyone running from them was VC and shoot at them. So the journalists stood and watched as the plane dropped a bomb filled with napalm, a sticky, flammable substance that, once ignited, can reach 5,000 degrees Fahrenheit.

Nick focused his camera. He was struck with the fierce beauty of the bomb's colorful explosion, which covered the highway and the fields in smoke. He wished at that moment that his camera contained color film.

Then he felt the bomb's intense heat, even though he was standing hundreds of yards away. It felt, he thought, "as if a door had opened on an immense brick furnace."

The next thing he noticed were screams. They came from inside the smoke.

"People have been bombed!" yelled a Peace Corps worker in the group of journalists.

Out of the smoke emerged screaming women and children running toward the journalists, who snapped photo after photo as they approached.

Then came a naked, screaming girl. Her name was Kim Phuc, and she was nine years old.

When the second plane dropped its napalm, Kim became engulfed in flames. Her clothes burned off. Her left arm was on fire. When she tried to brush the flames with her right hand, it became engulfed in the same burning sensation covering her neck and back.

She heard her brother's voice and tried to follow it. She stumbled through the smoke screaming: *"Nong qua, nong qua!"* (Too hot, too hot!)

Nick saw her. As she approached with her brothers in front of her, he snapped a photo. Then he tried to help. He heard the girl asking for water. He repeated her request to whoever could hear him. An ARVN soldier held his canteen to her lips. Other ARVN soldiers emptied their canteens over her back. Nick covered her with a poncho, put her in the news van, then took her and another burned woman to a Saigon hospital.

Then he rushed to have his film developed. On the following day, June 9, 1972, the photo of screaming, naked Kim Phuc running down the road with other casualties of war made the front pages of newspapers worldwide. It would win Nick multiple international prizes, including the American Pulitzer.

Two days after the attack, reporters Christopher Wain and Michael Blakey tried to track Kim down. They found her unconscious at the First Children's Hospital in Saigon. When they asked a nurse how the girl was doing, the woman answered, "Oh, she die, maybe tomorrow, maybe next day."

Clearly no one was fighting to save the girl's life. Christopher and Michael called the American embassy and asked if Kim could be transferred to an American hospital. Yes, said the embassy official, but only if the South Vietnamese foreign ministry gave the OK.

But the official at the foreign ministry hesitated. The transfer might make his government look bad, he said.

Christopher couldn't believe what he was hearing. "The entire world has just seen the South Vietnamese air force bombing the hell out of their own people, and this would make it worse for you?" he said.

The official agreed to the transfer, and from that day on, Kim received better care.

She had suffered severe burns over 30–35 percent of her body and remained in critical care for a month. The treatment to save her life—daily cleansing in a burn-case bathtub—was horrifically painful to the wounded little girl. Her father stayed at her side night and day; he wanted to be there when she died so he could take her body home.

But Kim didn't die. After a 14-month stay at the American hospital, she was finally strong enough to return to her war-ravaged home. The Associated Press Bureau in Saigon was inundated with gifts and money intended for "the little girl in the picture." Nick Ut did what he could to make sure Kim's father received his daughter's gifts.

Kim with Nick Ut in 1973.
Associated Press

In January 1973 German photojournalist Perry Kretz was under house arrest in a Saigon hotel. His crime? Photographing an ARVN soldier asleep at his post. But before Perry's visa expired, he was determined to get one more story. He bribed his guard and walked two blocks to the Associated Press office. There he spoke with Peter Arnette, a New Zealand journalist who had won the 1966 Pulitzer Prize for his war reporting. Perry asked Peter if he had any ideas for a good story.

"Kim Phuc is a good story," said Peter.

"Who's Kim Phuc?" asked Perry.

"She's the girl burned by napalm."

Perry was incredulous. "She's alive?!"

Perry traveled to her house and took photographs of her. When they walked to the spot where Kim had been hit by the napalm, her smile faded. Was she experiencing bad memories, Perry wondered. No, she told him. It was the heat. The damaged portions of her skin—which now contained no pores or sweat glands—had just overheated.

They returned to the house, and while the little girl cooled off with a shower, Perry, with the family's permission, took photos of Kim's scarred back. Then he returned to Germany, and his article was published. But he couldn't get Kim out of his mind.

And Kim couldn't get free of the war. There were still occasional incidents during which she had to run for her life because of shelling. In recurring nightmares, she was always running, running, running away from danger. She just wanted the war to end.

On April 30, 1975, it finally did. That morning her uncle Thieu "called for silence" as he tried to hear the news broadcasting from his transistor radio. General Duong Van Minh, Thieu said, was surrendering to the Communists. All South Vietnamese soldiers were to lay down their weapons.

"It's over," said Thieu. "The war is over."

The children cheered. The adults wept. "We lost, we lost, we lost," they said. Their sorrow was justified: Kim's father and uncle were soon sent to so-called reeducation camps because the new government had decided they needed to be indoctrinated with Communist ideology. They were released several years later and, like thousands of others Southern Vietnamese people who survived the reeducation camps, returned mere ghosts of their former selves.

The years passed, and during Kim's final year of high school, she decided on a career in medicine, partly because she remembered the kind doctors and nurses who had worked to save her life. But when she took the pre-entrance university exam, she came two points short of the standard that would allow her into medical school. She would have to take a six-month course in Tien Giang in order to prepare for university work.

On the day in April 1981 when Kim was ushered out of her math class to assure four important-looking men that she was the famous girl in the picture, they seemed surprised. "But, you look very—*normal!*" said one.

Kim understood. She drew up the sleeve on her left arm. It was covered with scar tissue.

The men left, apparently satisfied they had found the right girl. Kim returned to her classroom, slightly amused but also puzzled. Why the search for her, and why now?

Two days after Kim completed her premedical course and returned home, she began to understand. The same men appeared at her home in a van. They said they were taking Kim to Ho Chi Minh City (Saigon's new name since 1976) to see their "boss." They didn't give her a reason.

When they arrived at their destination, the Information Ministry, an official and writer for the *Communist Daily* gave Kim an explanation. A German journalist had been looking for her, he said, and had requested the assistance of the Vietnamese government. "He met you 10 years ago and could not forget you." The government decided to help the journalist and ordered a search for Kim.

A Vietnamese official escorted Kim to a hotel, where she met with three foreign journalists. They asked her what she remembered of the napalm attack and what she had been doing since. Then she was treated to the most extravagant meal she had ever eaten.

Kim was invited to two more interviews with foreign journalists that summer. She didn't understand why she was being treated like a celebrity, but she enjoyed the attention, even though talking about the napalm attack brought on vivid nightmares.

She was more than ready to put it all behind her, especially when she passed the entrance exam for medical school and moved to Ho Chi Minh City in October to begin her studies.

She was thrilled to have a good future ahead of her, unlike many young people in the South: children of families who had served the Southern government in any way were not allowed to attend professional schools

But to Kim's great disappointment, the meetings with Western journalists did not stop. During her first week of medical school, she was summoned from her classroom once per week for interviews in Tay Ninh, a province northwest of Ho Chi Minh City. The man who initiated these interviews was a Communist official in his late 50s named Hai Tam. He was undereducated, with only two years of formal schooling, but had been rewarded for his loyal support of the Communist cause during the war with this high-level job.

Each week Tam would invite Western journalists to his office, where he would lecture them on Socialism before allowing them to interview Kim. After each reception, Tam took Kim aside and angrily corrected her on whatever he believed she had said incorrectly. He told her she could say anything about her napalm wounds but nothing that might be perceived as negative about Vietnam's current government.

After each session, Kim had to find her own transportation from Tay Ninh back to Ho Chi Minh City. Once she asked Tam if she could hitch a ride with the foreign journalists. Tam refused, and Kim knew better than to ask again.

By November, the interviews had increased to twice per week. The minders—that is, the men in charge of collecting Kim for the interviews—were rude and inconsiderate. Sometimes they made her sleep on a cot outside Tam's office the night before an interview. Kim became increasingly anxious about all the classes she was missing. She did her best to borrow notes from fellow students, but she couldn't make up necessary hours spent in the laboratory, clinics, and hospitals.

She tried to protest, but it did no good. She asked one journalist why they were all so interested in her story. "You are 'hot' news," he said.

Finally, the inevitable happened. The dean of the medical school told her she would have to drop out.

Heartbroken, Kim pleaded with him to change his mind.

It was impossible. The officials in Tay Minh claimed Kim had become too important and that Ho Chi Minh City was no longer safe for her, he said.

Kim went to see Tam, and he confirmed her suspicions: he had been behind the dean's decision.

"You cannot go to Ho Chi Minh City to study," he said. "You are an important victim of the war. I want you here. Your job is to answer the telephone and type for me."

Kim tried to run away, but when Tam threatened to harm her parents, she went along with his wishes. Interested in learning English, she signed up for a language course in Ho Chi Minh City, but her parents, sinking under ever-growing taxes, couldn't afford to pay her tuition.

The interviews became more frequent. One of the journalists who came to see her was Perry Kretz. Kim was glad to see him again, but she lied about what she was doing, as she did to all the journalists. Tam had ordered her to pretend she was still a medical student. A Dutch film made at the time actually showed her in a classroom with other medical students. In reality, Kim avoided her fellow students as much as possible; they were now beginning their second year of studies, and she didn't want to be overwhelmed with jealously.

They have destroyed my life. Why do they do this to me? Why? Kim asked herself one day.

Her physical and emotional health were both deteriorating, but she couldn't receive the specialized care related to her scar tissue—which still caused intense intermittent pain and exhaustion—because her family wasn't Communist. But perhaps she could do something about her growing depression, she thought. Longing to feel happy again, she tried to seek a oneness with God through a renewed devotion to the faith she was raised in—Caodai, a Vietnamese religion that combines elements of Confucianism, Taoism, and Buddhism. But her acceptance of her current situation—perhaps the result of sins in her past lives, she thought—and her intense prayers did nothing to alleviate the downward spiral of her emotions. So she went to her library and carefully studied a variety of texts from different religions. She eventually converted to Christianity, discovering in it the inner peace she had been craving. Then she prayed for someone to rescue her. Perry Kretz came immediately to mind.

She wrote him a letter asking for help, knowing very well that if the letter fell into the wrong hands, she and her whole family might be arrested.

Perry received her letter and said to his publishers, "We've run her picture and done stories on her many times. Why don't we do something for her?"

The Vietnamese government allowed him to take Kim to Germany, where she received several operations that greatly eased the pain from her scar tissue.

During this visit, Kim became famous all over again. At a reception at the Vietnamese embassy in Germany, she trusted a kind-looking official with her story, how she was being forced to live a lie. He put her in touch with Vietnam's prime minister, Pham Van Dong, a kind man, he said, who had been a personal friend of Ho Chi Minh.

When Kim returned to Vietnam and met Prime Minister Pham Van Dong, he took pity on her and had the government pay her tuition to study English in Cuba. While there Kim fell in love with another Vietnamese student, Bui Huy Toan. They married in 1992 and planned to spend their honeymoon in the Soviet Union. But when their plane stopped in Canada to refuel, Kim and Toan remained behind, seeking—and gaining—asylum in that country.

Kim was finally free.

In 1997 she was named a goodwill ambassador for UNESCO, the United Nations Educational, Scientific, and Cultural Organization. That same year, she created the Kim Foundation International, a nonprofit organization whose mission is to provide medical and psychological care to children in war situations.

LEARN MORE

Fire Road: The Napalm Girl's Journey Through the Horrors of War to Faith, Forgiveness & Peace by Kim Phuc Phan Thi (Tyndale Momentum, 2017).

"The Girl in the Picture: Kim Phuc's Journey from War to Forgiveness" by Paula Newton, CNN, June 25, 2015, www.cnn.com/2015/06/22/world/kim-phuc-where-is-she-now/index.html.

The Girl in the Picture: The Story of Kim Phuc, the Photograph, and the Vietnam War by Denise Chong (Penguin Books, 2001).

Kim Phuc Foundation website, www.kimfoundation.com.

ACKNOWLEDGMENTS

IT WAS THRILLING TO WRITE a book that put me in direct contact with so many history makers. My gratitude to the following women for our clarifying and rewarding communications: Geneviève de Galard de Heaulme, Le Ly Hayslip, LCDR (Ret.) Bobbi Hovis, Jurate Kazickas, Anne Koch Voigt, Xuan Phuong, Kay Wilhelmy Bauer, and Tracy Wood. Many thanks to the Buckley family for providing the images of Lynda Van Devanter and to the Vietnam Women's Museum in Hanoi for providing images of Dang Thuy Tram.

I was completely overwhelmed when Diane Carlson Evans agreed to write the foreword, and I get chills every time I read it. Thank you, ma'am, for your wartime service and all you've done for women veterans since.

The following people—all cognizant adults during the Vietnam War—were kind enough to offer me their valuable time, answering a multitude of questions and reading portions of the book: the brilliant and well-read Bob Blomquist, who reviewed the general introduction; Brian Flora, Vietnam veteran and retired diplomat, who read all the introductory materials; and Dr. Robert Messer, associate professor emeritus of 20th-century history at the University of Illinois at Chicago, who reviewed the entire manuscript and who, I'm very proud to say, pronounced it an A– before his corrections.

Chicago Review Press, thank you for your enthusiastic green light. Specific gratitude to: Lisa Reardon, for skillfully helping me launch the proposal; Lindsey Schauer and Ellen Hornor, for their brilliant editorial suggestions; and Sarah Olson, for her beautiful cover design.

GLOSSARY

Army of the Republic of Vietnam (ARVN) The fighting force allied
with the Americans against the Vietnamese Communists, who were
waging guerrilla warfare in the South against them.

Democratic Republic of Vietnam The name Ho Chi Minh gave to
Vietnam when he declared its independence from France on September 2, 1945. When the nation split in two, this is what the Northern
half was called until 1976, when the North and South were officially
united under the name the Socialist Republic of Vietnam.

Indochina A term created in the early 19th century to describe a geo-
graphic location later referred to collectively as Vietnam, Cambodia,
and Laos.

National Liberation Front (NLF) A political organization founded in
1960 to overthrow the Republic of Vietnam (South Vietnam) and its
allies in order to unify the nation.

North Vietnamese Army (NVA) A term created by the Americans
to distinguish these Northern soldiers from the People's Liberation
Armed Forces (PLAF), known to their enemies in the South as the
Vietcong (VC). The actual term for the NVA was Quain Doi Nhan
Dan Viet or the People's Army of Vietnam, the same term used to
refer to the army of present-day Vietnam.

People's Army of Vietnam (PAVN) or Quain Doi Nhan Dan Viet Nam
The name of the army of present-day Vietnam. During the First
(French) Indochina War, it was referred to by outsiders as the Vietminh. During the Second (American) Indochina War, it was referred
to by the Americans as the North Vietnamese Army (NVA).

People's Liberation Armed Forces (PLAF) The fighting force of the
National Liberation Front (NLF), this was the official name of the
Vietnamese Communists in the South who were fighting against the
Army of the Republic of Vietnam (ARVN) and their American allies.

Provisional Revolutionary Government (PRG) The government created by the National Liberation Front on June 8, 1969, in order to provide Southern Communists with a diplomatic presence at the peace
talks. When the Vietnamese Communists defeated the Army of the
Republic of Vietnam on April 30, 1975, the PRG became the provisional government of South Vietnam until it merged with North Vietnam the following year to form the Socialist Republic of Vietnam.

Republic of Vietnam The state that existed south of the 17th parallel in
Vietnam from 1955 to 1975.

Socialist Republic of Vietnam The name of united Vietnam since 1976.

Vietcong (VC) Short for Viet Nam Cong San, or Vietnamese Communist, this was a derogatory name for the soldiers of the People's Liberation Armed Forces (PLAF). The term was created by their enemies
in the Southern government, the Republic of Vietnam, to distinguish
them from the Vietminh, who were respected by the Vietnamese
people for defeating the French during the First Indochina War.

Vietminh An abbreviation of Viet Nam Doc Lap Dong Minh, the Vietnam Independence League, a fighting force that existed briefly in the
1930s but was revived in 1941 to organize resistance to the French and
Japanese occupiers.

NOTES

INTRODUCTION

"I want to rail": Stanley Karnow, *Vietnam: A History—the First Complete Account of Vietnam at War* (New York: Viking, 1983), 100.

1.1 million Communist combatants: Encyclopedia Britannica, s.v. "Vietnam War," www.britannica.com/event/Vietnam-War.

2.5 million Vietnam veterans: Tom Valentine, "Vietnam War Veterans," the Vietnam War, April 7, 2014, http://thevietnamwar.info/vietnam-war-veterans/.

58,000 American Vietnam War veterans: Encyclopedia Britannica, s.v. "Vietnam War," www.britannica.com/event/Vietnam-War.

PART I: 1945-1956

"All men are created equal": "Declaration of Independence of the Democratic Republic of Vietnam," History Matters, http://historymatters.gmu.edu/d/5139/.

"will of heaven": Frances Fitzgerald, *Fire in the Lake: The Vietnamese and the Americans in Vietnam* (Boston: Little, Brown, 1972), 24.

"twice sold our country": "Declaration."

"You can kill": Stanley Karnow, *Vietnam: A History—the First Complete Account of Vietnam at War* (New York: Viking, 1983), 183.
Ninety thousand French soldiers: Karnow, *Vietnam*, 188.

XUAN PHUONG

"The Japanese have": Phuong Xuan and Danièle Mazingarbe, *Ao Dai: My War, My Country, My Vietnam* (New York: EMQUAD International, 2004), 50.
"From this day": Xuan and Mazingarbe, *Ao Dai*, 53–54.
"French soldiers": Xuan and Mazingarbe, *Ao Dai*, 58.
"Why are you crying?": Xuan and Mazingarbe, *Ao Dai*, 106.
"Nothing we had heard": Xuan and Mazingarbe, *Ao Dai*, 129.
"The atmosphere": Xuan and Mazingarbe, *Ao Dai*, 131.
"We work one": Xuan and Mazingarbe, *Ao Dai*, 134.
"Why are you living" . . . *"Phuong, why don't you"*: Xuan and Mazingarbe, *Ao Dai*, 142.
"I never could": Xuan and Mazingarbe, *Ao Dai*, 148.
"You people have": Xuan and Mazingarbe, *Ao Dai*, 163.
"No, I want to look" . . . *"What have all"*: Xuan and Mazingarbe, *Ao Dai*, 167.
"for the good": Xuan and Mazingarbe, *Ao Dai*, 174.
"I had spent": Xuan and Mazingarbe, *Ao Dai*, 237.

GENEVIÈVE DE GALARD

"From the air": Geneviève de Galard, *The Angel of Dien Bien Phu: The Sole French Woman at the Decisive Battle in Vietnam* (Annapolis, MD: Naval Institute Press, 2010), 39.
"I felt as if" . . . *"The shelling lasted"*: Galard, *Angel*, 56.
"care for and stay": Galard, *Angel*, 57.
"performed miracles": Galard, *Angel*, 61.
"What do you know?": Galard, *Angel*, 76.
"when wounded, the toughest": Galard, *Angel*, 62.
"Every time you walk": Galard, *Angel*, 63.
"the soul and mind" . . . *"that astonishing offer"*: Galard, *Angel*, 78.
"Geneviève has earned": Galard, *Angel*, 80.
"terrifying noise" . . . *"The battle was now"*: Galard, *Angel*, 82.
"I shared with" . . . *"The fighting would cease"*: Galard, *Angel*, 83.
"were all close to tears" . . . *"strange silence"*: Galard, *Angel*, 84.
"columns of French prisoners": Galard, *Angel*, 85.

approximately 9,000: Martin Windrow, *The Last Valley: Dien Bien Phu and the French Defeat in Vietnam* (Cambridge, MA: Da Capo, 2006), 624.

300 miles away, the other 450: Windrow, *Last Valley*, 638.

3,900 of the original 9,000: Windrow, *Last Valley*, 647.

"Since you speak": Galard, *Angel*, 86.

"Were you scared?": Galard, *Angel*, 111.

"I haven't earned this honor": Galard, *Angel*, 119.

"have suffered so much": Galard, *Angel*, 141.

Excerpts from Geneviève de Galard, *The Angel of Dien Bien Phu: The Sole French Woman at the Decisive Battle in Vietnam* (Annapolis, MD: Naval Institute Press, 2010) used by permission of Naval Institute Press.

PART II: 1957-1964

90 percent: Stanley Karnow, *Vietnam: A History—the First Complete Account of Vietnam at War* (New York: Viking, 1983), 227.

1,500 US military personnel: George G. Herring, *America's Longest War: The United States and Vietnam, 1950–1975* (New York: McGraw-Hill, 1996), 62.

"barbeques": Herring, *America's Longest War*, 106.

LE LY HAYSLIP

"French come": Le Ly Hayslip with Jay Wurts, *When Heaven and Earth Changed Places: A Vietnamese Woman's Journey from War to Peace* (New York: Doubleday, 1989), 3.

"even the friendly": Hayslip, *Heaven and Earth*, 3.

"Freedom is never": Hayslip, *Heaven and Earth*, 30.

"Do these things": Hayslip, *Heaven and Earth*, 33.

"Your children need": Hayslip, *Heaven and Earth*, 37.

"that traitor": Hayslip, *Heaven and Earth*, 35.

"We are the soldiers": Hayslip, *Heaven and Earth*, 37.

"whining and flapping" . . . *"The may bay chuong-chuong"*: Hayslip, *Heaven and Earth*, 43.

"After a while": Hayslip, *Heaven and Earth*, 69.

"Where did you": Hayslip, *Heaven and Earth*, 77.

"Didn't we arrest": Hayslip, *Heaven and Earth*, 80.

"Are you so smart": Hayslip, *Heaven and Earth*, 201.

Excerpts from Le Ly Hayslip with Jay Wurts, *When Heaven and Earth Changed Places: A Vietnamese Woman's Journey from War to Peace* (New

York: Doubleday, 1989) copyright © 1989 by Le Ly Hayslip and Charles Jay Wurts. Used by permission of Doubleday, an imprint of the Knopf Doubleday Publishing Group, a division of Penguin Random House, LLC. All rights reserved.

BOBBI HOVIS

"[The] waterways appeared": Bobbi Hovis, *Station Hospital Saigon: A Navy Nurse in Vietnam, 1963–1964* (Annapolis, MD: Naval Institute Press, 1992), 14.
"anti-American feelings": Hovis, *Station Hospital*, 15.
DUONG DUONG: Hovis, *Station Hospital*, 33.
"From the day": Hovis, *Station Hospital*, 32.
"The demand for": Hovis, *Station Hospital*, 40.
"At intersections": Hovis, *Station Hospital*, 58.
"I have never": Hovis, *Station Hospital*, 61.
"He proceeded to": Hovis, *Station Hospital*, 64.
"The abnormal was": Hovis, *Station Hospital*, 65.
"There's all kinds": "Coup in Saigon: A Nurse Remembers," *Navy Medicine* 88, no. 6 (November–December 1977): 16.
"tree limbs snapping": Hovis, *Station Hospital*, 78.
"uneasy" . . . *"could explode"*: Hovis, *Station Hospital*, 83.
"The hourly news": Hovis, *Station Hospital*, 83.
"showered with flying": Hovis, *Station Hospital*, 84.
"Ironically": Hovis, *Station Hospital*, 84.
"the clank, clank, clank": "Coup," 20.
"were blackened" . . . *"pounding headaches"*: Hovis, *Station Hospital*, 86.
"had holes": Hovis, *Station Hospital*, 86.
"assassination": Hovis, *Station Hospital*, 91.
"the war effort": Hovis, *Station Hospital*, 93.
"Two Americans a Day": Hovis, *Station Hospital*, 112.
"I had never seen": Hovis, *Station Hospital*, 114.
"twisted metal" . . . *"cold chill"*: Hovis, *Station Hospital*, 115–116.
"saturation point" . . . *"were among"*: Hovis, *Station Hospital*, 130.
"The care of": Aries Matheos, "Around Annapolis: 1st Navy Nurse Corps Officer to Volunteer for Vietnam Honored by DAR," *Capital (MD) Gazette*, October 31, 2014, www.capitalgazette.com/neighborhoods/ph-ac-cc-around-annapolis-1031-20141031-story.html.
Excerpts from Bobbi Hovis, *Station Hospital Saigon: A Navy Nurse in Vietnam, 1963–1964* (Annapolis, MD: Naval Institute Press, 1992) used by permission of Naval Institute Press.

PART III: 1965-1968

exceeds 100 million: www.hawaii.edu/powerkills/COM.ART.HTM.

"there was no more": Frank Kusch, *Battleground Chicago: The Police and the 1968 Democratic National Convention* (Westport, CT: Praeger, 2004), 43

"an honorable end": www.youtube.com/watch?v=5HBON-ZIyUE.

KAY WILHELMY BAUER

"Kay, just a minute": Kay Bauer, "Catherine (Kay) M. Bauer," in *Vietnam War Nurses: Personal Accounts of 18 Americans*, ed. Patricia Rushton (Jefferson, NC: McFarland, 2013), 11.

"I think so" . . . *"There's a &%$+"*: Bauer, "Catherine," 11.

"I was so surprised": Bauer, "Catherine," 19.

"Wait a minute": Bauer, "Catherine," 19.

"Are you LCDR Bauer?": Kay Bauer, e-mail correspondence with author, February 14, 2016.

"'Wrong House' idea": Kay Bauer personal papers (article title and date unknown).

"We have just unveiled": Diane Carlson Evans, Vietnam Women's Memorial unveiling speech, November 11, 1993.

"overwhelmed by the number": Kay Bauer, interview with author, December 2, 2016.

"The VAMC at that time": Bauer interview, December 2, 2016.

JURATE KAZICKAS

"Everything we have done": Jurate Kazickas, "These Hills Called Khe Sanh," in *War Torn: Stories of War from the Women Reporters Who Covered Vietnam*, Tad Bartimus et al. (New York: Random House, 2002), 124.

"raging fires that": Kazickas, "These Hills," 123.

"crazy, terrifying": Kazickas, "These Hills," 126.

"Something was planted": Kazickas, "These Hills," 126.

"elephant": Kazickas, "These Hills," 128.

"Hardcore!": Kazickas, "These Hills," 130.

"Watching them kidding": Kazickas, "These Hills," 128.

"What's a woman like you": Kazickas, "These Hills," 124.

"You mean you came" . . . *"My country was taken"*: Kazickas, "These Hills," 125.

"journalistic fraternity" . . . *"What the hell"*: Kazickas, "These Hills," 133.

"War, for all its": Kazickas, "These Hills," 135-136.

"Don't worry, man" . . . *"The moment was"*: Kazickas, "These Hills," 140.

"terrifying visions" . . . *"Without the companionship"*: Kazickas, "These Hills," 142.

"American soldiers were": Kazickas, "These Hills," 136.

"What are they": Kazickas, "These Hills," 143.

"the unmistakable": Kazickas, "These Hills," 144.

"subliminal pull" . . . *"I seemed inexorably"*: Kazickas, "These Hills," 149.

"Getting wounded": Kazickas, "These Hills," 150.

"passionate about" . . . *"memories with a vengeance"*: Kazickas, "These Hills," 151.

"one frantic night" . . . *"We thought you"*: Kazickas, "These Hills," 151–152.

Excerpts from Jurate Kazickas, "These Hills Called Khe Sanh," in *War Torn: Stories of War from the Women Reporters Who Covered Vietnam*, Tad Bartimus et al. (New York: Random House, 2002) used by permission of International Creative Management, Inc.

IRIS MARY ROSER

"I walked off": Iris Mary Roser, *Ba Rose: My Years in Vietnam, 1968–1971* (Sydney: Pan Books, 1991), 9.

"Don't you know" . . . *"But unlike them"*: Roser, *Ba Rose*, 12.

"Unfortunately, you have": Roser, *Ba Rose*, 14.

"through the village": Roser, *Ba Rose*, 23.

"Go! Go!": Roser, *Ba Rose*, 24.

"Their gratitude for": Roser, *Ba Rose*, 33.

"to appease their gods": Roser, *Ba Rose*, 34.

"Hello, Mrs. Water Buffalo": Roser, *Ba Rose*, 35.

"expecting a burst": Roser, *Ba Rose*, 47.

"Charlie" . . . *"a dark head"*: Roser, *Ba Rose*, 62.

"Ong Krah, he is coming!": Roser, *Ba Rose*, 64.

"I wondered": Roser, *Ba Rose*, 65.

"How stupid can you": Roser, *Ba Rose*, 66.

became *"Ba [Mrs.] Rose"*: *Ba Rose*, 94.

"Who are the recipients" . . . *"a link in"*: Roser, *Ba Rose*, 95.

"When we entered": Roser, *Ba Rose*, 103.

"She was afraid": Roser, *Ba Rose*, 104.

"In sum, here is": Roser, *Ba Rose*, 287.

Extracts from Iris Mary Roser, *Ba Rose: My Years in Vietnam, 1968–1971* (Sydney: Pan Books, 1991) reprinted by permission of Pan Macmillan Australia Pty Ltd. Copyright © Iris Mary Roser 1991.

PART IV: 1969-1970

eventually igniting a third World War: David F. Schmitz, *Richard Nixon and the Vietnam War: The End of the American Century* (Lanham, MD: Rowman & Littlefield, 2014), 5.

accusations flowing as freely as the French wine: Richard Burks Verrone and Laura M. Calkins, *Voices from Vietnam: Eye-Witness Accounts of the War, 1954–1975* (Exeter, UK: David & Charles, 2005), 269.

"the great silent majority" . . . *"The defense of freedom"*: "Silent Majority," Nixon Presidential Library and Museum, www.nixonlibrary.gov /forkids/speechesforkids/silentmajority.php.

"for the purpose": Schmitz, *Nixon*, 89.

"might be on": "Richard M. Nixon: Address to the Nation About a New Initiative for Peace in Southeast Asia—October 7, 1970," American Presidency Project, www.presidency.ucsb.edu/ws/?pid=2708.

ANNE KOCH

"Ooh, blood!": Anne Koch Voigt, e-mail correspondence with author, November 2, 2015.

"It was quite a shock!": Voigt e-mail, November 14, 2015.

"I knew in my heart": Voigt e-mail, November 14, 2015.

"I don't know why" . . . *"the fastest"*: Voigt e-mail, November 14, 2015.

"A Poem for Anne Koch": Anne Koch Voigt papers.

"We would smile": Voigt e-mail, November 14, 2015.

"Cowboys and Indians" . . . *"can happen in"*: Voigt e-mail, November 14, 2015.

"I never forgot the care": Anne Koch Voigt papers.

"There was nothing different": Voigt e-mail, November 14, 2015.

"just-in-case blood": Voigt e-mail, November 14, 2015.

"wide-eyed" . . . *"I knew they were"*: Voigt e-mail, November 14, 2015.

"Soon he became" . . . *"shocked and upset"*: Voigt e-mail, November 14, 2015.

"short-time calendar" . . . *"I had the wrong"*: Voigt e-mail, November 18, 2015.

"Class As" . . . *"I haven't done anything"*: Voigt e-mail, November 18, 2015.

"You always knew": Voigt e-mail, November 18, 2015.

"It may not have": Voigt e-mail, November 18, 2015.

DANG THUY TRAM

"This year greater": Dang Thuy Tram, *Last Night I Dreamed of Peace: The Diary of Dang Thuy Tram*, trans. Andrew X. Pham (New York: Harmony Books, 2007), 79–80.

"*Our responsibility is*": Dang, *Last Night*, 22.
"*My clearest feeling*": Dang, *Last Night*, 55.
"*I have a physician's*": Dang, *Last Night*, 20.
"*Greetings, Doctor!*": Dang, *Last Night*, 82.
"*Oh, Bon*" . . . "*Hatred for*": Dang, *Last Night*, 83.
WAITING FOR YOU . . . "*crimes committed*": Dang, *Last Night*, 99–100.
"*free-fire zones*": Dang, *Last Night*, 103n97.
"*It's not yet 8:30*" . . . "*between ragged breaths*": Dang, *Last Night*, 112–113.
"*the roar of planes*": Dang, *Last Night*, 119.
"*the intensity of*" . . . "*a maelstrom*": Dang, *Last Night*, 120–121.
"*Where each bomb*" . . . "*From a position*": Dang, *Last Night*, 135.
"*eerily empty*" . . . "*If the enemy comes*": Dang, *Last Night*, 140–141.
"*Perhaps I will meet*": Dang, *Last Night*, 146.
"*soaking wet and shivering*": Dang, *Last Night*, 160.
"*Death is close*": Dang, *Last Night*, 172.
"*Trees downed in every*": Dang, *Last Night*, 215.
"*Don't burn this one*": Dang, *Last Night*, xvi.
"*What agony!*": Dang, *Last Night*, 41.
"*struggle for national salvation*": Charles E. Neu, ed., *After Vietnam: Legacies of a Lost War* (Baltimore: Johns Hopkins University Press, 2000), 89.
1.5 million . . . *60,000*: Karen Gottschang Turner with Phan Thanh Hao, *Even the Women Must Fight* (New York: John Wiley & Sons, 1998), 20.
Excerpts from Dang Thuy Tram, *Last Night I Dreamed of Peace: The Diary of Dang Thuy Tram*, trans. Andrew X. Pham (New York: Harmony Books, 2007), translation copyright © 2007 by Andrew X. Pham, used by permission of Harmony Books, an imprint of the Crown Publishing Group, a division of Penguin Random House, LLC. All rights reserved.

LYNDA VAN DEVANTER

"*Those guys*" . . . "*I think you're both*": Lynda Van Devanter with Christopher Morgan, *Home Before Morning: The Story of an Army Nurse in Vietnam* (New York: Beaufort Books, 1983), 49.
"*Essentially, we were deciding*": Van Devanter, *Home*, 68.
"*jerking wildly*": Van Devanter, *Home*, 76.
"*Men, we just came*" . . . "*But if there*": Van Devanter, *Home*, 77.
"*Coiled barbed wire*" . . . "*supposedly unending*": Van Devanter, *Home*, 78.
"*There were only fifteen*": Van Devanter, *Home*, 82.
"*A blur of wounded*" . . . "*slow period*": Van Devanter, *Home*, 85.
"*the war was*": Van Devanter, *Home*, 87.

"Attention all personnel": Van Devanter, *Home*, 90.
"How do you know": Van Devanter, *Home*, 91.
"The moans and screams": Van Devanter, *Home*, 96.
"You're a good help": Van Devanter, *Home*, 104.
"Trying to sound" . . . *"Nobody does"*: Van Devanter, *Home*, 105.
"At 4:16 a.m.": Van Devanter, *Home*, 113.
"Let the old glory mongers": Van Devanter, *Home*, 131.
"as a warning": Van Devanter, *Home*, 132.
"in Vietnam to save": Van Devanter, *Home*, 134.
"It would be a lot easier": Van Devanter, *Home*, 139.
"Holding the hand" . . . *"If you can't feel"*: Van Devanter, *Home*, 144.
"They were all with me": Van Devanter, *Home*, 173.
"freedom flight" . . . *"As the jet"*: Van Devanter, *Home*, 207.
"We're going past the airport" . . . *"that naïve"*: Van Devanter, *Home*, 211.
"less gruesome" . . . *"I had learned"*: Van Devanter, *Home*, 221.
"Lynda's book": "Vietnam Veterans of America Mourns the Loss of Lynda Van Devanter," Leatherneck.com, www.leatherneck.com/forums/showthread.php?2495-Vietnam-Veterans-Of-America-Mourns-The-Loss-Of-Lynda-Van-Devanter&s=e0131ddd162ce635538f29d7c0e9b3be.
Excerpts from Lynda Van Devanter with Christopher Morgan, *Home Before Morning: The Story of an Army Nurse in Vietnam* (New York: Beaufort Books, 1983) used by permission of the Buckley family.

PART V: 1971–1975

"morally wrong": Christian G. Appy, *Patriots: The Vietnam War Remembered from All Sides* (New York: Penguin Books, 2004), 393.
"search-and-avoid": Brian Flora, Vietnam veteran, interview with author, January 6, 2017.
"Why did you let us win?": Tom Bissell, *The Father of All Things: A Marine, His Son, and the Legacy of Vietnam* (New York: Pantheon, 2007), 91.
"repeatedly and in massive": "Gerald R. Ford: The President's News Conference—April 3, 1975," American Presidency Project, www.presidency.ucsb.edu/ws/?pid=4812.
"Yes, we defeated": Stanley Karnow, *Vietnam: A History—the First Complete Account of Vietnam at War* (New York: Viking, 1983), 9.
"I didn't want to be measured": Chad Stewart, "Former POW, Ambassador, Shares His Unique Perspective on Vietnam," *On Patrol*, summer 2014, http://usoonpatrol.org/archives/2014/08/13/former-pow-ambassador-shares-h.

KATE WEBB

"It was simply": Kate Webb, "Highpockets," in *War Torn: Stories of War from the Women Reporters Who Covered Vietnam*, Tad Bartimus et al. (New York: Random House, 2002), 61.

"seriously hungry": Webb, "Highpockets," 62.

"function and write": Webb, "Highpockets," 64.

"political clamor": Webb, "Highpockets," 70.

"dragging war" . . . "the tiny phosphorous": Webb, "Highpockets," 69.

"engulfed in chaos": Webb, "Highpockets," 71.

"No": Webb, "Highpockets," 72.

"fire burst from all sides": Kate Webb, *On the Other Side: 23 Days with the Viet Cong* (New York: Quadrangle Books, 1972), 9.

"April 8": Webb, *Other Side*, 13.

"Nha bao" . . . "Nuoc": Webb, "Highpockets," 73–74.

"That the others": Webb, "Highpockets," 74.

"I tasted it" . . . "compulsive documenting": Webb, "Highpockets," 74.

"slipped like shadows": Webb, "Highpockets," 76.

"As our numbers": Webb, "Highpockets," 75.

"Do not be afraid": Webb, *Other Side*, 47.

"Why were you down" . . . "Now I wish": Webb, "Highpockets," 76.

"Why were you with" . . . "too long": Webb, *Other Side*, 49.

"An odd thing happened": Webb, "Highpockets," 75–76.

"the gray limbo" . . . "Hope, we had learned": Webb, "Highpockets," 78.

"liberated": Webb, "Highpockets," 79.

"Mad Hatter's tea party" . . . "humane treatment": Webb, *Other Side*, 141–142.

"stood alone in the dark": Webb, "Highpockets," 79.

"Kassat, kassat": Webb, *Other Side*, 152.

"Miss Webb": Webb, *Other Side*, 153.

"bizarre mixture": Webb, "Highpockets," 79.

"a field reporter" . . . "what was happening": Webb, "Highpockets," 84–85.

"There were suicides": Webb, "Highpockets," 85.

"fearless action reporter": Douglas Martin, "Kate Webb, War Correspondent, Dies at 64," *New York Times*, May 15, 2007.

Excerpts from Kate Webb, "Highpockets," in *War Torn: Stories of War from the Women Reporters Who Covered Vietnam*, Tad Bartimus et al. (New York: Random House, 2002) used by permission of International Creative Management, Inc.

JOAN BAEZ

"quit meddling around": Joan Baez, *And a Voice to Sing With: A Memoir* (New York: Summit Books, 1987), 117.

"a quiet revelation" *"disaster"*: Baez, *And a Voice*, 119.

"Well, I imagine": Baez, *And a Voice*, 121.

"filled with young men": Baez, *And a Voice*, 123.

"Do not kill" . . . *"Yes, it's right"*: Joan Baez, *Daybreak* (New York: Dial, 1966), 87.

"I will not bring myself": Baez, *Daybreak*, 85.

"alert": Baez, *And a Voice*, 201.

"look at Nixon's peace": Baez, *And a Voice*, 208.

"terrible" . . . *"end real soon"*: Baez, *And a Voice*, 212.

"What I mean is": Baez, *And a Voice*, 213.

"My son, my son": Baez, *And a Voice*, 218.

"Instead of bringing hope": Joan Baez, "Open Letter to the Socialist Republic of Vietnam," *New York Times*, May 30, 1979, A14.

Joan Baez Gave Comfort . . . *"You know"*: "Waydownsouth," "Joan Baez Diffuses Right Wing Protest at Idaho Concert," *Daily Kos*, August 12, 2009, www.dailykos.com/story/2009/08/12/765667/-Joan-Baez-diffuses -right-wing-protest-at-Idaho-concert.

TRACY WOOD

"When do I leave" . . . *"If anything happened"*: Tracy Wood, "Spies, Lovers, and Prisoners of War," in *War Torn: Stories of War from the Women Reporters Who Covered Vietnam*, ed. Tad Bartimus et al. (Random House, 2002), 224.

"Landry had just": Wood, "Spies," 225.

"You're too feminine" . . . *"Don't become like"*: Wood, "Spies," 228.

"I couldn't let this happen": Wood, "Spies," 228.

"You don't want anything" . . . *"Cowboys"*: Wood, "Spies," 229.

"Well, we can't tell Arthur": Wood, "Spies," 230.

"We're only reporters": Wood, "Spies," 227.

"Bribery was so commonplace": Tracy Wood, "A War Correspondent Turned Lifelong Corruption Fighter," *Voice of Orange County*, April 29, 2015, http://voiceofoc.org/2015/04/a-war-correspondent-turned -lifelong-corruption-fighter/.

"I lost all sensation": Wood, "Spies," 232.

"a massive hammering" . . . *"His left hand"*: Wood, "Spies," 234.

"A cease-fire, internationally": "Richard M. Nixon: Address to the Nation Announcing Conclusion of an Agreement on Ending the War and Restoring Peace in Vietnam—January 23, 1973," American Presidency Project, www.presidency.ucsb.edu/ws/?pid=3808.

"something in their posture": Wood, "Spies," 244.

"nagged by" . . . *"They had no identity"*: Wood, "Spies," 245.

"Is that really Walter Cronkite" . . . *"the Most Trusted"*: Wood, "Spies," 246.

Excerpts from Tracy Wood, "Spies, Lovers, and Prisoners of War," in *War Torn: Stories of War from the Women Reporters Who Covered Vietnam*, Tad Bartimus et al. (Random House, 2002) used by permission of International Creative Management, Inc.

KIM PHUC

"You are Kim Phuc?": Denise Chong, *The Girl in the Picture: The Story of Kim Phuc, the Photograph, and the Vietnam War* (New York: Penguin Books, 2001), 190.

"big attack": Chong, *Girl*, 53.

"Everybody get out!" . . . *"Run!"*: Chong, *Girl*, 60.

"even more off target": Chong, *Girl*, 61.

"as if a door had opened": Chong, *Girl*, 63.

"People have been": Chong, *Girl*, 64.

"Nong qua, nong qua!": Chong, *Girl*, 68.

"Oh, she die": Chong, *Girl*, 80.

"The entire world": Chong, *Girl*, 80.

"the little girl in the picture": Chong, *Girl*, 106.

"Kim Phuc is a good story": Chong, *Girl*, 108–109.

"called for silence" . . . *"We lost, we lost"*: Chong, *Girl*, 137.

"But, you look very": Chong, *Girl*, 190.

"boss" . . . *"He met you"*: Chong, *Girl*, 197.

"You are 'hot' news": Chong, *Girl*, 203.

"You cannot go to Ho Chi Minh City": Chong, *Girl*, 205.

"They have destroyed": Chong, *Girl*, 212–213.

"We've run her picture": Chong, *Girl*, 228.

BIBLIOGRAPHY

Titles marked with an asterisk are particularly suited to young readers.

BOOKS

Appy, Christian G. *Patriots: The Vietnam War Remembered from All Sides.* New York: Penguin Books, 2004.

Baez, Joan. *And a Voice to Sing With: A Memoir.* New York: Summit Books, 1987.

Baez, Joan. *Daybreak.* New York: Dial, 1966.

Bartimus, Tad, et al. *War Torn: Stories from the Women Reporters Who Covered Vietnam.* New York: Random House, 2002.

Bauer, Kay M. "Catherine (Kay) M. Bauer." In *Vietnam War Nurses: Personal Accounts of 18 Americans,* edited by Patricia Rushton, 11–21. Jefferson, NC: McFarland, 2013.

Bissell, Tom. *The Father of All Things: A Marine, His Son, and the Legacy of Vietnam.* New York: Pantheon, 2007.

Bradley, Doug, and Craig Werner. *We Gotta Get Out of This Place: The Soundtrack of the Vietnam War.* Amherst: University of Massachusetts Press, 2015.

Caputo, Philip. *A Rumor of War.* New York: Holt, Rinehart and Winston, 1977.

*Caputo, Philip. *10,000 Days of Thunder: A History of the Vietnam War*. New York: Atheneum Books for Young Readers, 2005.

Chanoff, David, and Doan Van Toai. *Portrait of the Enemy: The Other Side of Vietnam, Told Through Interviews with North Vietnamese, Former Vietcong and Southern Opposition Leaders*. New York: Random House, 1986.

Chong, Denise. *The Girl in the Picture: The Story of Kim Phuc, the Photograph, and the Vietnam War*. New York: Penguin Books, 2001.

Dang, Thuy Tram. *Last Night I Dreamed of Peace: The Diary of Dang Thuy Tram*. Translated by Andrew X. Pham. New York: Harmony Books, 2007.

Elliott, Duong Van Mai. *The Sacred Willow: Four Generations in the Life of a Vietnamese Family*. New York: Oxford University Press, 1999.

Fall, Bernard B. *Hell in a Very Small Place: The Siege of Dien Bien Phu*. Cambridge, MA: Da Capo, 1966.

FitzGerald, Frances. *Fire in the Lake: The Vietnamese and the Americans in Vietnam*. Boston: Little, Brown, 1972.

*Freedman, Russell. *Vietnam: A History of the War*. New York: Holiday House, 2016.

Galard, Geneviève de. *The Angel of Dien Bien Phu: The Lone French Woman at the Decisive Battle for Vietnam*. Annapolis, MD: Naval Institute Press, 2010.

Green, Bob. *Homecoming: When the Soldiers Returned from Vietnam*. New York: G. P. Putnam's Sons, 1989.

Hajdu, David. *Positively 4th Street: The Lives and Times of Joan Baez, Bob Dylan, Mimi Baez Farina, and Richard Farina*. New York: Farrar, Strauss and Giroux, 2001.

Hall, Simon. *Peace and Freedom: The Civil Rights and Antiwar Movements of the 1960s*. Philadelphia: University of Pennsylvania Press, 2005.

Hayslip, Le Ly, with James Hayslip. *Child of War, Woman of Peace*. New York: Doubleday, 1993.

Hayslip, Le Ly, with Jay Wurts. *When Heaven and Earth Changed Places: A Vietnamese Woman's Journey from War to Peace*. New York: Doubleday, 1989.

Heikkila, Kim. *Sisterhood of War: Minnesota Women in Vietnam*. St. Paul: Minnesota Historical Society Press, 2011.

Herring, George C. *America's Longest War: The United States and Vietnam, 1950–1975*. New York: McGraw-Hill, 1996.

Hoffmann, Joyce. *On Their Own: Women Journalists and the American Experience in Vietnam*. Cambridge, MA: Da Capo, 2008.

Hovis, Bobbi. *Station Hospital Saigon: A Navy Nurse in Vietnam, 1963–1964.* Annapolis, MD: Naval Institute Press, 1992.

Karnow, Stanley. *Vietnam: A History—the First Complete Account of Vietnam at War.* New York: Viking, 1983.

Kazickas, Jurate. "'These Hills Called Khe Sanh." In *War Torn: Stories of War from the Women Reporters Who Covered Vietnam*, Tad Bartimus et al., 121–153. New York: Random House, 2002.

Kusch, Frank. *Battleground Chicago: The Police and the 1968 Democratic National Convention.* Westport, CT: Praeger, 2004.

Neu, Charles E., ed. *After Vietnam: Legacies of a Lost War.* New York: Johns Hopkins University Press, 2000.

Roser, Iris Mary. *Ba Rose: My Years in Vietnam, 1968–1971.* Sydney: Pan Books, 1991.

Schmitz, David F. *Richard Nixon and the Vietnam War: The End of the American Century.* Lanham, MD: Rowman & Littlefield, 2014.

*Sheinkin, Steve. *Most Dangerous: Daniel Ellsberg and the Secret History of the Vietnam War.* New York: Roaring Brook, 2015.

Steinman, Ron. *Women in Vietnam: The Oral History.* New York: TV Books, 2000.

Taylor, Ethel Barol. *We Made a Difference: My Personal Journey with Women Strike for Peace.* Philadelphia: Camino Books, 1998.

Townley, Alvin. *Defiant: The POWs Who Endured Vietnam's Most Infamous Prison, the Women Who Fought for Them, and the One Who Never Returned.* New York: Thomas Dunne Books, 2014.

Truong, Nhu Tang, with David Chanoff and Doan Van Toai. *A Vietcong Memoir: An Inside Account of the Vietnam War and Its Aftermath.* New York: Harcourt, Brace, Jovanovich, 1985.

Turner, Karen Gottschang, with Phan Thanh Hao. *Even the Women Must Fight: Memories of War from North Vietnam.* New York: John Wiley & Sons, 1998.

Xuan, Phuong, and Danièle Mazingarbe. *Ao Dai: My War, My Country, My Vietnam.* New York: EMQUAD International, 2004.

Van Devanter, Lynda, with Christopher Morgan. *Home Before Morning: The Story of an Army Nurse in Vietnam.* New York: Beaufort Books, 1983.

Verrone, Richard Burks, and Laura M. Calkins. *Voices from Vietnam: Eye-Witness Accounts of the War, 1954–1975.* Exeter, UK: David & Charles, 2005.

Walker, Keith. *A Piece of My Heart: The Stories of Twenty-Six American Women Who Served in Vietnam.* Novato, CA: Presidio, 1985.

Webb, Kate. "Highpockets." In *War Torn: Stories of War from the Women Reporters Who Covered Vietnam*, Tad Bartimus et al., 61–89. New York: Random House, 2002.

Webb, Kate. *On the Other Side: 23 Days with the Viet Cong*. New York: Quadrangle Books, 1972.

Wildwind, Sharon Grant. *Dreams That Blister Sleep: A Nurse in Vietnam*. Edmonton, AB: River Books, 1999.

Windrow, Martin. *The Last Valley: Dien Bien Phu and the French Defeat in Vietnam*. Cambridge, MA: Da Capo, 2006.

Wood, Tracy. "Spies, Lovers, and Prisoners of War." In *War Torn: Stories of War from the Women Reporters Who Covered Vietnam*, Tad Bartimus et al., 223–249. New York: Random House, 2002.

Zaroulis, Nancy, and Gerald Sullivan. *Who Spoke Up? American Protest Against the War in Vietnam 1963–1975*. New York: Holt, Rinehart, and Winston, 1984.

ARTICLES AND WEBSITES

"Coup in Saigon: A Nurse Remembers." *Navy Medicine* 88, no. 6 (November–December 1977): 16–21. https://archive.org/details /NavMedicineVol.88No.6November-december1997.

Olson, Wyatt. "40 Years After Release, POWs at Hanoi Hilton Reflect on Experience." *Stars and Stripes*, February 10, 2013. www.stripes.com /news/pacific/40-years-after-release-pows-at-hanoi-hilton-reflect-on -experience-1.207382.

"Richard Nixon: Address to the Nation About a New Initiative for Peace in Southeast Asia—October 7, 1970." American Presidency Project. www.presidency.ucsb.edu/ws/?pid=2708.

Steward, Chad. "Former POW, Ambassador, Shares His Unique Perspective on Vietnam." *On Patrol*, summer 2014. http://usoonpatrol .org/archives/2014/08/13/former-pow-ambassador-shares-h.

"Vietnam War Veterans." The Vietnam War. http://thevietnamwar .info/vietnam-war-veterans/.

Wood, Tracy. "A War Correspondent Turned Lifelong Corruption Fighter," Voice of Orange County, April 29, 2015. http://voiceofoc.org /2015/04/a-war-correspondent-turned-lifelong-corruption-fighter/.

RECORDINGS

Baez, Joan. *Where Are You Now, My Son?* Pickwick Records: 1973.

INDEX